IF IT WEREN'T FOR THE ALLIGATORS

ROWDY YATES

Rowdy Yates was born in 1950 in the Lake District, where he enjoyed "probably one of the last wireless and short-pants childhoods in the U.K." After a "somewhat wild" career in his early teens, he returned to the family trade; as a wood-cutter in the Western Isles. A chance encounter led him to a very different career in the drugs field with the Lifeline Project, for whom he has worked, in a variety of capacities, for the last 21 years. He has lectured widely on drugs and addiction both in the U.K. and throughout Europe, West Africa and the U.S.A.

If It Weren't For The Alligators
Copyright © R. Yates 1992.

**British Library Cataloguing In
Publication Data.**

*A Catalogue Record for this Book is available
from The British Library.*

ISBN 0 9520082 0 3 Paperback.

*Published by Lifeline Project Limited 1992,
Globe House, Southall Street, Manchester M3 1LG*

*Printed by East Cheshire Printing Co. Ltd.
Cover Design by Reactor.
Cover Photograph by Kathleen Yates.*

To all those drug users who have known me; and l, them.
I have tried, in my way, to be of some use to you. I hope l have
been no harm.

ACKNOWLEDGEMENT

This book is dedicted to all those drug users who have come into contact with the Lifeline Project over it's twenty-one years.

But it could never have been written without the strength and support of those who have worked for the organisation; whether paid or not. Nor without the belief and support of our many funders over the years.

Special thanks are due to Paul Flowers, our current Chair, who suggested the theme; to Kathleen, my wife, who listened, uncomplaining to my limited store of anecdotes; to my sons, Christy and Calum, who rejuvenated my interest in Rupert, Toad and the Thunderbirds, without which, this book would lack much of its flavour; to Michael Linnel for the illustrations; and to James Muir Morrison for reading the first drafts, making many helpful suggestions and for correcting my spelling and grandma.

CONTENTS

FOREWORD

All things being equal, twenty-first birthday parties for those being lucky enough to afford them, are a significant notch in a young persons right of passage. That point when Dad pats you on the back, points to the Yellow Brick Road and wishes you well of life's hard trek. Unfortunately, all things aren't equal and the survival of the Lifeline Project, in this, its twenty-first year bears testimony to that.

This book written by its present Director, Rowdy Yates, is a smashing chronicle of the project from its inception. What is peculiarly riveting about his translation of events is the way it is interwoven with recent social history. This rather idiosyncratic style, which reflects the author's personality, gives the book its power and its pathos. While the reader gets off on the heady days of sex, drugs and rock 'n' roll, the author introduces unblocking the airway of a punter who has recently overdosed. Although the subject and content of this book will possibly evoke a "Reading that will only depress me" attitude in potential purchasers, this isn't the case. The "let it all hang loose" approach of the author is enough to not only have you doubled up, but almost peeing yourself with laughter. This is best illustrated when the project was so into its heavy therapy period that one potential punter chose to go to prison for three years rather than enter it. Any project that can laugh at itself in this way is the sort of place that has matured by learning from its mistakes. One is left in no doubt that Lifeline and the people who run it have made a tremendous contribution in helping many people with drug problems. After reading this account of its survival I was left feeling angry at our politicians for their failure to establish a Lifeline Project in every one of our major cities.

JIMMY BOYLE

PREFACE

" I said my lovely Creole girl
My money it is no good
If it weren't for the alligators
I'd sleep out in the wood
You're welcome in kind stranger
Our house is very plain
But we've never turned a stranger out
On the lakes of Ponchatrain"

Traditional American
from
'The Lakes of Ponchatrain'

PREFACE

"Any writer, no matter how modest", said Logan Pearsall Smith, "hides within himself an outrageous vanity; chained like a madman to the walls of the padded cell of his heart". Chekhov, I think, held a similar view of the inherent egotism of the author. Thus, (as they say), ran my thoughts when it was first suggested to me that I should set down a personal chronicle of my involvement with the Lifeline Project.

Actually this is a blatant untruth, but I wanted to ensure that there was a really big whopper on the first page. My father always told me to start off as I meant to go on. In fact, I have only vaguely heard of Logan Pearsall Smith and had certainly never read any of his work. I only came across his words by accident, whilst I was hunting through a dictionary of quotations, looking for something quite different. Still, it does read a good deal better than my own immediate response:-

"Bloody hell. Give over. Who'd want to read about my life?".

But, after very tentatively asking around, it did appear that there might be some small market for such a publication. On this basis, I prepared the business plan, mapped out my expected sales against my fixed costs, mapped out both against my variable costs, and estimated that the project would be viable provided I sold the finished books at two hundred and fifty pounds each. Since I estimated that this was roughly equal to about seventy-five Barbara Cartlands or fifty Jeffrey Archers, I reckoned I was onto a good thing.

You will find a great deal in this book about the extraordinary events which took place amongst (mainly) young people in the United Kingdom during the 1960's. At first sight, this might seem strange in a book which considers the history of an organisation - and my part within it - which only began in 1971. But the dramatic flowering of youth culture during that period; the birth of rock 'n' roll, and beat, and psychedelic music were the outward manifestations of a movement, of sorts, which genuinely believed in its capacity to change the structure of society.

However great the temptation to scorn the naivety of those beliefs, it remains true that those of us who were young at that time, believed these things almost without question. It felt, then, as if anything were possible. We did not question the notion of an alternative society; we simply jigged up and down with excitement; hardly able to contain ourselves, waiting for it to come. It never did. Gradually, bit by bit the momentum was swallowed up by what we called 'straight' society. In part, during the process, society did change a little. But mainly, it was us who did the changing; who adapted; conformed.

The poster for M.A.G.I.C. was based on a Tarot Card. Much of our symbolism was influenced by Ley Lines; much of our thinking echoed the alternative dream of the 'sixties.

But such a momentous upheaval, (and this was a momentous upheaval; a party that lasted for a whole decade), could not disappear entirely. In music and popular culture, its impact remains obvious, tangible. In other areas, it is more difficult to identify. The Lifeline Project which began in Manchester in 1971, grew out of this culture (or counter-culture). This was its heritage. Lifeline, Release in London, MAGIC (Manchester Alternative General Information Centre) in Manchester, Kirkintilloch Arts Lab in Glasgow, and many more. These were not of the voluntary sector. These were the field hospitals of the counter-culture revolution. Some, like Lifeline, remained behind after the armistice was declared to care for the wounded, the displaced, the lonely.

The change and growth from such beginnings into an organisation, almost - not quite, but almost - in the mainstream of voluntary sector welfare provision was, perhaps, understandably slow; certainly, predictably painful.

This is not a history book. I have tried to convey some of what it felt like to be a part of that process. I wanted to give at least some impression of what we aspired to do, rather than just what we actually did. For if truth be told, we often had very little idea of, or even control over, the direction in which we were going. Often, I think, we were groping around in the dark. Alone. Speaking in slogans. Dream dancing. Embarrassed, or frightened of awakening our fellow slumberers. Stubbing our toes in the pitch black. Gripping our barked shins and hissing under our breath.

But for all our mistakes, I believe that we have a history we can be proud of. If I appear to cast a jaundiced eye over our history (and, some would say, prehistory), it is simply because I think that some of our mistakes were, in retrospect, uproariously funny. Or tragically sad. And we can, surely, talk of our faults without damning our achievements. Erich Honecker, former beloved leader of the German Democratic Republic, did not hesitate, in his recent memoirs, to point the finger at the shortcomings of his former administration. "We did not always", he writes, "have enough bananas". So now you know.

As for my own part in this history, I really am not so convinced that it has been of such significance. My chief contribution, perhaps, has been longevity. I have gained a great deal from the Lifeline Project over the years I have been involved with it. The Project has become very personalized for me. Much of the stumbling about in the dark has been my own stumbling about in the dark. Many of the mistakes have been mine, entirely. Some of the good ideas, I can lay claim to. But, in the end, I took some decisions which brought the organisation credit, which accelerated its progress. I also took some decisions which retarded it. Stopped it dead in its tracks. It is not for me to say whether I have been good for Lifeline. I don't even know whether Lifeline has been good for me. What is significant, I believe, is that the organisation has continued to grow despite

Dr. Eugenie Cheesmond at the door of the original Day-Centre at 81 Moseley Street; now part of Manchester's prized collection of empty office blocks.

whatever any individual might do within it.

And the credit for that must surely lie, not with me, not with any of the other workers, not with the volunteers, nor with the management committee; but with the customers.

They have borne of our fumblings for the truth; for solutions. Their resilience and good humour has limited our excesses and encouraged our successes. It is they, and not our bright ideas, not market forces, not the supply of drugs, not the emergence of AIDS, who have dictated our progress. They are the ones who have bowed to our missionary zeal, suffered our encounter groups, and, in the last analysis, voted with their feet when we got it wrong. We, in contrast, have simply responded.

This is not a history book. It does not follow a chronological pattern. Each chapter deals with a different aspect of my/our history. Some examine popular culture and drug use; some, politics and organisational growth. Others are about therapy, or music, or anything else that took my fancy at the time. If you have been around and involved in the organisation during this period, don't expect to find yourself in these pages. Don't flip to the index; there isn't one. All the customers featured in this book have been given false names. For them, this will not be a new experience. The only other named individual in these pages is Lifeline's founder; Eugenie Cheesmond. It was her dream which established the Project. That dream has been carried forward by myself and others. I hope that we have done it justice.

The story, I believe, is worth telling if only because many now simply don't believe that there was life before 1984 and the sudden explosion of drug treatment services. For a long time we had the road to ourselves. We pottered along in our Morris Traveller, stopping every now and then to take in the views. Then suddenly, from nowhere, the road was alive with Ford Sierras. History is little more than a catalogue of grotesque accidents. We have rarely managed to learn from history and hardly ever adjusted our progress accordingly. But, it might just be that if you come across an old Morris which has driven down the same road a few years earlier only to find itself crossing bumpers with a brick wall: well, it might just be that the wall is still there and you should slow down. Or maybe check out another route. Sad then, that so many Sierra drivers have thrown away their rear view mirrors on the basis that nothing behind us is going fast enough to worry about.

As with any other endeavour, much of what we now consider to be basic about working with drug users, has been won, against the odds and at enormous cost, by a small number of individuals and organisations. Their legacy is surely worthy of our consideration.

The title of this book comes from a traditional American folk song describing an incident at the end of the Civil War. A former soldier arrives at the Lakes of Ponchatrain with nothing in his pocket but a roll of, now worthless, Confederate currency. There, he is shown great kindness and becomes consumed with a passion. The rest of his life is to be illuminated by an icon. Somewhat fanciful, perhaps, but the words of the song were rolling around my mind for much of the time it took to write this book. I too, arrived in a strange place with the wrong currency. A place I was never able to think of as home. I too, became taken up with an idea; a belief. And it has dogged my footsteps for twenty-one years.

This book is the story of what happened. I hope it is truthful. I hope it is kind to its characters. And I hope it provides some food for thought.

I hope you enjoy the story. But listen. If you don't, don't come running to me for your two hundred and fifty quid back.

CHAPTER ONE

IN OUT OF THE RAIN

"In Dublin next arrived and thought it such a pity
To be so soon deprived a view of that fair city
So then I took a stroll all amongst the quality
Me bundle it was stolen in a neat locality
Something crossed me mind and when I looked behind
No bundle could I find upon me stick a bobbling
And 'quiring for the rogue they said me Connaught brogue
Wasn't very much in vogue on the rocky road to Dublin"

Traditional Irish
from
'The Rocky Road to Dublin'

IN OUT OF THE RAIN

Late summer in 1971 was, as I remember, very hot. On the streets of Manchester there was a proliferation of young women in halter-tops, mini-skirts and those extraordinary platform-soled high heels. Similar footwear had found favour with young men also. Along with 'grandad' vests and voluminous flared trousers. To the unhip traveller it appeared that most of Manchester was populated by Minnie Mouse and Sailor Jack from the Rupert Annual.

Platform-soled high heels were probably first worn by Roman emperors. They called them buskins. They believed that the heel was the most holy part of the emperor's most holy body. They made sure it never touched the ground. This was the meaning of the wings on the heels of Mercury. The Hun did not go in for buskins. They favoured short axes and goatskin slippers. They chopped the Roman Empire to pieces and trod all over it. The discount clearance warehouses of Rome must have been piled high with buskins. Throughout history, at its most gullible moments someone, somewhere manages to off-load some of that surplus stock. The moment is never long. In 1971 it lasted little more than a year. The counter-culture alternative society was already fizzling out. Already throughout much of England, all that remained were a few rarefied pockets of hip capitalism. The world had gone a little mad. Now it was coming to again. The big hit that year was Middle of the Road with "Chirpy Chirpy Cheep Cheep". Life goes on.

Halfway round the world the socialist administration of Dr. Allende shocked the world of western capital by announcing the de facto nationalisation of Chile's banks. This had been achieved by the simple expedient of quietly - often through intermediaries - buying up stock. By September 1971 the government had a controlling interest in all the country's major banks. Formal nationalisation, they announced, (I imagine, with something of a smirk), was no longer necessary. It was an artifice which was bound to infuriate the right.

History is little more than a catalogue of grotesque accidents. On Dr. Allende's list, this was one written in bold type. Within two years, it was to lead to his death in an American-inspired and financed coup that was to deliver Chile into the hands of a military dictatorship for the next two decades. In the first days, in the gigantic football stadium in Santiago, Victor Jara, the prominent singer-songwriter of the left was brutally executed. As if to emphasise the juxtaposition of politics and art, the guitar player's fingers on both hands were systematically broken by the Army's torture squad before he was beaten, torn with electric shocks and, finally, shot. Thus came together in a single bloody act two of the three elements which were to play such an important part in the shaping of my life: politics and music.

Politics and music. These two had been my bedfellows for some years. But

RELEASE ACT AGAINST POLICE

Head Fuzz busted

This poster has been issued by Release as their latest, and most public attempt to bring to popular notice the corruption that they allege exists within the police force, and in particular the Drugs Squad.

Every point on the poster has emerged from the testimony of Detective Chief Inspector Victor Kelaher, formerly of the Scotland Yard Drug Squad, but now in an administrative job. He is a prosecution witness in a trial of five people charged with conspiracy to acquire unlawfully imported cannabis.

Rufus Harris, Caroline Coon's co-administrator on Release, says: 'Although this whole affair has been known for months to top officials — both in the police and at the Home Office — as well as the press, nothing has been done about it. We have put out this poster at the end of four years of trying to get allegations of police corruption properly investigated.'

Although Release have repeatedly approached the Home Office with detailed complaints, the affair in question has until now been either whitewashed or ignored. Police attitudes have always been negative.

'Even when we published the "Release Report" in 1968,' says Caroline Coon, 'no-one wanted to know. 'I was called into the Yard, ostensibly to discuss youth liaison, and was hauled up in front of one of the biggest men there. He told me that the book was inaccurate, that it was quite probably libellous, and that I should make a public apology for it.'

The police also mentioned that if any other cases did come up, then they should be sure to bring them forward, and they would be dealt with at once. When a bribery case emerged within two weeks of Caroline's interview, Release duly reported it to the authorities. Nothing was done.

'We aren't looking for "success" like the police look for convictions,' says Harris. 'But we do want to get proper investigations carried out.' Police rejection of Release allegations is carried. According to Caroline, 'There are Home Office drugs inspectors who are passing on information to their superiors and who have told us that they're very worried when no action is being taken. The last Home Secretary was overprotective of the police, and it doesn't appear that this one is any different.'

By alleging so openly what authorities and press have known in private for several months, Release hope to highlight for the public why so many young people have no faith in the police — 'Look at Kelaher. He admitted in court that he was quite willing to watch a 19-year-old girl go off to the Lebanon, score heroin and then bust her when she returned to England.

'We hope that this poster causes a rumpus,' says Caroline. 'And if it does, it will serve Scotland Yard right for failing to put their house in order. We have the duty to guarantee the people who come to us that there will be redress against police activities. The whole reason why we were raided last January (by impatient activists) was because we weren't radical enough.' 'Release have got to take action. Someone has to get something done before people become much more political and police activities like those at Reading Festival don't get accepted so passively. Otherwise there'll be riots outside the police stations.'

The case in which Kelaher's alleged malpractice has emerged is currently being heard at Middlesex Quarter Sessions. Already in progress for three weeks, it is expected to go on for at least as many more. Release expect that their poster will be brought into court and that at the least an enquiry should result — 'This time there's got to be action.'

MANCHESTER: NEW DRUG TREATMENT CENTRE

A day centre with a drug-free policy has opened in Manchester to provide for young addicts and anyone else in need of the facilities it offers.

Located at 81 Mosley Street in rooms that once belonged to the evangelistic coffee house The Catacombs, the centre is open though not yet fully operational. Those in charge are still taking out the pews to soften the bible-peddling atmosphere.

The medical officer for the centre, called Lifeline Trust, is Dr Eugenie Cheesmond. She's the doctor who became a national figure last year when she was attached to the drug treatment centre at Macclesfield Hospital. While waiting for the centre to open, she allowed a number of young addicts (25 at one stage) to take up residence in her rented farmhouse. After refusing to obey a hospital order to evict them, she was suspended from the staff. Although she was reinstated later, her contract was not renewed at the end of last September.

Dr Cheesmond's experience at the Barn, as her farm was called, helped considerably in drawing up a concept for Lifeline Trust. Once the day centre is well and truly established she hopes that the Trust will be able to find accommodation for a community of about 30 addicts.

She is incensed at official methods of handling the drug problem, particularly among young people. She believes that when they aren't punitive, they're incompetent because they work on the principle of using substitute drugs to reconcile the addict to the same social situation that drove him to drugs in the first place.

Dr Cheesmond stresses that the centre and the home, when it is found, will NOT aim at repairing the wiring and sending the components back into the machine. Instead, emphasis will be on the fact that narcotic use is an extremely self-centred activity and the solution to it is a commitment to other people and their needs.

Among the services at the centre will be cheap food, psychological counselling, crafts training, non-judgmental problem listening, and bum trip rescue missions.

Present services for addicts in the North Midlands area consist of two limited hospital treatment centres, a Methodist hostel for eight men, and, of course, Borstal and prison.

Jeff Jones

The opening of the Lifeline Day-Centre is announced in Richard Neville's ill fated INK Magazine.

the third. Drugs too, had played a major role in my life. But this was only the beginning. Oh yes, drugs were to become the biggest, most consuming passion of all. Looking back now, it sometimes feels as if that was almost all there ever was.

The historian, George Santayana achieved fame (for a little longer than his Andy Warhol-stipulated fifteen minutes) for his remark: "Those who cannot remember the past are condemned to repeat it". Coleridge had come nearer to the truth a hundred years before with, "the light which experience gives is a lantern on the stern, which shines only on the waves behind us". And history is little more than a catalogue of grotesque accidents. Far from learning from the mistakes of the past, all that a study of history can deliver is a single, simple message: "Watch out for accidents!". A series of minor accidents - or at least coincidences - had brought me to Manchester for a short visit.

It had started with a trip to Glasgow where, I had heard, an old friend was visiting our former haunts. By the time I arrived he had already left for London, planning, like many others at that time, to hit the 'hippy trail' for Goa. I had a few weeks in hand and I decided to hitch-hike South. London, I thought, would provide a little fun. I spent 48 hours just outside Hamilton waiting for a lift. By the time my first lift stopped, I'd already given up the chase. It was a fish lorry from Mallaig heading for the markets of Smithfield in Manchester. Manchester was another old haunt. My parents lived just outside the city. Manchester, I thought, would provide a little fun. After 48 hours on the kerbside at Hamilton, I would have been prepared to believe that Milton Keynes could offer a modicum of entertainment. The sun was just coming up as we rattled and roared into the streets of Granadaland. The starlings had just swept into the city out of the fields of Cheshire and were strung along the telegraph wires like pegs on a clothes line. Two days later, I found myself in a threadbare, brashly painted room in a building in the city centre.

The room had a high Victorian ceiling. The architraves, had been painted emperor purple. The walls, perversely, were bedecked in a combination of primrose yellow and shocking pink. Don't let anyone tell you any different. Whatever else the counter-culture might have delivered in terms of art and 'new' thinking, it had been disaster time for those who cared for colour and colour-match. Here in this room, the colours screamed at each other like parrots in a pet shop. The furniture had seen better days. Years maybe. Centre-stage in the room was an enormous shipping clerks desk. Behind the desk was an earnest young man. (I mean no harm. We were all earnest then. They were serious times). He was struggling with my banal questions; I was struggling to understand. Why, I asked, did drug users keep coming back. To me it seemed that there must be somewhere better. Everything it seemed - from making the tea to painting a room - was a therapeutic exercise. But I was at a loss to understand how these activities could be therapeutic within the Lifeline Project and mind-numbingly boring chores anywhere else. The difference, it seemed was therapy. But here I was in an alien landscape. He talked to me of groupwork, but the only groups I'd ever come across had bass, rhythm, lead and drums: and it had never looked like work. In fact, I still nurtured a dream of becoming a professional musician myself. It always looked such an easy way of making a living.

There is a condition known as 'white-out' which is common amongst those who work for extended periods in snow-covered landscapes. Just occasionally, the mind suddenly becomes confused and finds it impossible to interpret the information the eyes are providing. That five-inch line immediately ahead could be a twenty-foot high cliff two miles away. It could just as easily be a gaping chasm just before your feet. All the mind can register is a black line across a white background. Usually, white-out disappears almost as quickly as it appears. Closing your eyes for a few minutes can often do the trick. For me that afternoon, the confusion refused to go away. Words like groupwork, counselling, therapy, failed to dispel the white mists. There seemed to be no logical reason why young drug takers should continue to return to these shabby and depressing rooms day after day; in large numbers. The existence of a free midday meal appeared to provide some of the answer: I reached out, groping for it. But it was quickly snatched away. That too, it seemed, was a therapeutic exercise.

"Yes. We have a formal meeting every morning to decide who should cook; what it should be; who's washing up, and that sort of thing. Most of the people who come here have never had that sort of responsibility; have never had that sort of control over their lives. So we see it as a first step in a therapeutic journey which leads eventually towards a goal. Of being a whole person again without drugs".

(There have been times in my life when I have been convinced that I was definitely going mad).

"What, this lot?"

I jerked a thumb in the direction of the ragged band in the outer room. Beyond the pink and purple door, a squabble had broken out. Two of the group, both men, had lurched to their feet. There, in the middle of the room, they engaged in battle. More with gravity than each other. Mostly, they hurled invective at each other. A lot of this invective looked wet and whitish-green in colour. Battle lines had been drawn. *Somebody* must have had the last mandrax.

"Well, they've as much right to wholeness as anybody else!"

There was an unmistakable edge of irritation in his voice. I quickly tried to cover my tracks and erase any impression that I did not share his vision of wholeness, equality and the new world: above all, any impression that I might be

5

a 'straight'. ("Right on!" seemed to do the trick and, anyway, was the best I could manage in those less articulate days).

Thus mollified, he proceeded to map out for my benefit the Lifeline view of wholeness which appeared to contain a number of key elements; such as the right to burn joss sticks and play Roy Harper records at full volume without harassment by the police; the right to wear long hair (if you were a man) without attracting wolf-whistles from building site workers; and the right to explore your inner-self without the aid of chemicals. He could have gone on for hours - perhaps he did, I don't remember - but as soon as he had mentioned rights, I'd been hooked. We were all very big on rights in the early 'seventies and no-one was prepared to be the oppressor.

Lifeline Project had opened its day centre for drug users in Manchester some three months before and was now attracting fifty to sixty customers a day. I had spent some time in Manchester previously during an earlier and wilder career and was anxious to meet up with old friends from that period. Some discreet questioning over the previous two days had revealed that most would, by now, be Lifeline regulars.

And so there I was. Drinking in the New Word.

In fact, I actually did learn a new word that afternoon in late summer; and it was to alter my direction and shape my thoughts for the next twenty years. The word was therapy. It had mystery; it had excitement; and it had me by the nose.

As I left the building, one of the customers asked me for a cigarette. I paused; struggling with a difficult decision and quite sure that one of the workers would be watching me. Could giving a cigarette be seen as therapeutic, representing a first step towards developing a meaningful relationship which would eventually lead to his achieving - through me (of course) - wholeness? Or would it merely reinforce his feelings of low self-esteem? I decided on a compromise.

"You'll have to roll it yourself", I said, and passed him my tobacco pouch and papers.

It took about half-an-hour, during which time he managed to drop the best part of an ounce of tobacco down the side of an old, threadbare and extremely dirty armchair where even I recoiled from searching for it, and ruined a whole packet of papers by dropping it in his cup of tea. (The tea was then poured down the side of the armchair, thus eliminating any lingering hopes of recovering the tobacco).

When, eventually, I emerged into the late September sun it was with a sense that this might prove to be my most unusual holiday yet.

For the past few years, I had been working as a woodcutter, gardener and occasional deer-stalker in the Western Isles. I had made occasional forays to

Glasgow and had previously, for a short time, actually stayed in Manchester. But living full-time in the city was to be a shock to the system. On the morning of my arrival I almost wore myself out trying to say "good morning" to everyone in Market Street on the basis that where I had just come from you hailed anyone you met either because you knew them or because you didn't know them and they were therefore visitors to whom you had a duty of welcome. Now, having secured a flat, I found myself promptly burgled of most of my few possessions by the simple expedient of leaving my door open all day while I was out.

Before the two weeks were out, I had decided to move to Manchester permanently: or at least, as permanently as you might decide to do anything in your early twenties. My belongings were sent on to me by friends in Scotland. Of the two sea chests containing my clothing and books, only one ever materialised. My two chain saws and a set of axes arrived unboxed, courtesy of British Rail, and caused some little consternation in city-centre Manchester when I collected them from the station. Ironically, the rent on my bothy (cottage) was taken over by a poet and songwriter from Leeds who had decided, for the sake of his sanity, to abandon the city for the tranquillity of island life (I don't think he lasted the winter and I never saw any of his poetry published but, at the time, it seemed vaguely symbolic of something).

My days were settling into a pattern. During the week I set to, rebuilding the almost derelict building which Lifeline had rented from the City Council. And at the weekend I augmented my unemployment benefit by a little woodcutting work. Most of the latter was close-cutting - felling garden trees which were perilously close to their owners buildings. Inevitably, this took me to the more affluent areas; particularly Wilmslow and Alderley Edge, where they boast more swimming pools per square mile than any other part of Western Europe. For me, inevitably, the contrast was startling, obscene; and served to underline the sense of injustice which characterised my view of the work with Lifeline.

But I was enjoying my work with Lifeline immensely. There was, it is true, some dispute over whether my restoration work was to be seen as a 'therapeutic exercise' or not. For me this meant allowing drug users access to my tools (which I was convinced they would steal) and to the work itself (which I was convinced they would mess up), and I resisted it vigorously. But, by and large, I was left to my own devices to do the work as best I could, given the limited resources.

And here was the other major difficulty. There was no money. Lifeline had been established with a bank-balance of £151.00 and every job had to be funded by begging the materials or recycling old ones. All of this was very worthy and epitomised the Project at that time. But it did mean that even a small job, such as decorating an office, was apt to take weeks. I grew quite adept at telephone begging, although I suspect that the cost of the telephone calls sometimes

From "Drugs Through The Ages"
Smack In The Eye, Issue 4

outweighed the material benefits. But it didn't matter. Begging for things was part of the culture. It was political. 'Straight' society - and particularly business - owed drug users and the agencies which served them a debt of conscience. It was spiritually cleansing. Our poverty and unpopularity as a 'worthy cause' reinforced our view of ourselves as outside the establishment, creating an alternative and better society. It was therapeutic. Begging was how our customers survived too, and we believed it created a common bond.

Oh, and we were evangelists too. We spoke with fervour of the drug-ridden society. (Although our critique of society's drug use usually ignored tobacco and sometimes even alcohol). Society had been hypnotised by doctors and drug companies into accepting a chemical intervention for every unpleasant situation. It was a 'pill for all ills' society. Small wonder then, we said, that the young had taken to self-medication with such enthusiasm. We weren't entirely wrong. It was certainly true that prescriptions for sleeping pills, slimming pills and tranquillisers had rocketed in the post-war period. It was true, too, that had drug companies not been so motivated by profit margins, attention might have focussed on more socially useful medical research. Third world disease - leprosy, malaria and so on - was our particular favourite example. No, weren't wrong. But we couldn't see that the genie was out of the bottle and nothing we could do would push it back in. And our youthful fervour would not permit us to allow the possibility (at least that was how it was for me) that developments in medicine had, overall, been a powerful force for good.

Our guru in all this was an exotic and iconoclastic psychiatrist from South Africa. Eugenie Cheesmond had voluntarily ostracised herself from most of the medical profession and had established Lifeline with little more than her own intense personal commitment on the books. (Twenty-one years on, our balance sheet looks only marginally better.).

Eugenie's management style was autocratic and occasionally erratic. Of course, there were democratic conventions and protocols to observe but, by and large, Eugenie decided what we should do and we did it! Willingly. Usually with enormous enthusiasm. If she was anything, she was probably our mother. We rewarded her indulgence with an unflinching loyalty, hard work and the occasional temper tantrum.

Most of us were young. Most of us, in one way or another, products or survivors of the late 'sixties drug scene. There was little distinguishable difference between paid and unpaid workers. (And little, we hoped, between either group and our customers). Each of us took to the task in hand with unbridled - and, sometimes, wrong-headed - enthusiasm. When the money ran out in the first year, those of us who had been paid a small salary simply continued to work as before.

It did not occur to me for many months that I might fulfil any other role than that of day-centre handyman. The break-through came, I suppose, with my capacity to understand the broad, mandrax-slurred dialects of two Stirling-born drug users from Salford. It quickly became apparent that I was the only one who could make head or tail of what they were saying - or at least trying to say. I received my first promotion. I was the Projects first official interpreter.

These were not the days of equal opportunity. When a salary became available through the departure of one of the paid workers, I was informed that, as the longest serving volunteer, I would be given the job. I couldn't believe it. My grandmother had always fondly hoped that I might eventually "get a good job in a bank". This was not to say that working behind the counter in the Clydesdale Bank was regarded as something we should aspire to, but that, in my family, most of the work for men was outdoor; generally agricultural. 'Getting on' was seen not in terms of acquiring a high salary, but simply achieving an indoor job and getting in out of the rain.

But here I was, being offered just such an opportunity without any of the slog - no staying on at school, sitting exams, missing out on the vandalism in order to get the homework done and so on. Of course my grandmother never saw it that way. She remained to the end, bitterly disappointed that I never got a 'proper' job in a bank. When she died in 1987, I was Director of one of the UK's largest drug services, with a turn-over of nearly half a million pounds. But to her I remained a disappointment and on those odd occasions when I appeared on television, she was, I know, embarrassed and ashamed that everyone would see I was associated with "those people". Just think of that.

It had been agreed that I should start to be paid the inconsiderable sum of thirteen pounds a week from 1st April 1972; to be confirmed by a formal interview at a later date. I would have done it for sixpence. Apart from my obsession with the work, I had found the process of being registered unemployed humiliating and embarrassing. My initial inquisition at the Department of Employment had gone quite well at first. It had been patiently explained to me that qualifications would normally be required if I wanted to be a social worker. But, if I was really serious, unqualified social workers were sometimes taken on, mostly in the voluntary sector of course . . . . . In the end, it was my previous employment which proved my undoing. My innocent litany of woodcutter, fisherman, talisman, deer-stalker, gardener . . . provoked an angry response. "You're taking the piss aren't you?", said the exasperated employment benefit clerk; and threw down his pen in disgust.

My 'formal' interview for the Lifeline job eventually took place with one of the 'hipper' members of the Management Committee in the Bad Trip Tent at Bickershaw Festival around one o'clock on a very wet and dismal Saturday morning. At the other end of the tent another Lifeline worker was having her feet bathed and massaged by Brother Jeremy of the Mirfield Community. An act, I think, of outstanding Christian generosity.

I remember very little else about the Festival which was marred, for us, by a running battle with Release, who were encamped next-door for a similar purpose. They were all Londoners (soft Southerners, we affectionately dubbed them) and their putative leader was also called Jeremy. A fitting name for a monk perhaps. But for a drugs worker in the early 'seventies? I should cocoa! There was a lot of mud and dodgy LSD, I remember. Country Joe was there, without his Fish and Led Zeppelin made an appearance, I think. A somewhat emaciated looking old man dived from a high tower into a large water tank between the 'real' acts, without anybody really noticing. But for me, everything else was a blur. I was a social worker! It was official! Absurdly, I suppose now, I had been saving my thirteen pound wages, terrified that I would fluff the interview and be asked to pay it all back. I returned to work on the Monday with a renewed excitement. That week I sold my chain saws and axes.

CHAPTER TWO

DECADE DECAYED

"Each torpid turn of the world
has such disinherited children
to whom no longer what's been
and not yet what's coming belongs"

R.M. Rilke
from
'The Collected Works'

DECADE DECAYED

Somewhere around the turn of the century, people began to categorise history in terms of its decades. The 'roaring' 'twenties, the 'depressed' 'thirties, the 'swinging' 'sixties. Of course the swinging 'sixties didn't begin in 1960. Nor did they end in 1969. But the impact of the 'sixties continued to reverberate throughout the 'seventies. The 'suppurating' 'seventies were probably the longest wake in history. They were filled with the stench of the decay of the disintegrating counter culture. They were filled with the sound of the middle-class leaders of that revolution scuttling into 'proper' jobs; into the media, into publishing, into design houses, into a myriad of wholefood capitalist small enterprises. By the 'winter of discontent' in 1979, very little remained of the 'summer of love'.

Nobody could say now when the 'sixties counter culture really began. Perhaps it was in 1955 at the Troccadero Cinema, Elephant and Castle, with the first British showing of Bill Haley's 'Rock Around the Clock'. Perhaps in 1957, with the publication of Kerouac's 'On the Road'. Whenever it was, one thing is clear. It began in the art schools and universities of Cheltenham, Oxford, Cambridge. It's origins were never in Barnsley, Wigan or Birmingham. It started with the flourishing of small poetry magazines like 'Evergreen Review', 'New Departures', 'Tree'. It was consolidated by the Aldemaston Marches when the poets and the beats met the hordes from left-wing youth organisations and heard folk songs for the first time. And when the jazz freaks from Ronnie Scott's met up with the rastafarians in Notting Hill Gate and discovered cannabis. It was given its final polish when the Beatles released 'Please Please Me' during the Helen Shapiro tour for which they were the support act. By the end of the tour, poor Helen was walking back to obscurity.

The rallying cry was an obscure quotation from Plato; "When the mode of the music changes, the walls of the city shake". Not many working class kids had read Plato. This, at least remains the same.

Actually, it was almost certainly a mistranslation. What Plato actually said was: "When modes of music change the laws of the state always change with them". If we'd had *that* version, some of us might have seen the Dangerous Drugs Act coming. Some of us might have seen the 'OZ' trial looming. In fact, the literary and cultural pretensions of the counter-culture often fell flat on their face in the guano. The logo for 'International Times' (IT) *the* seminal 'underground' newspaper of the 'sixties, was intended to be a clever theatrical pun. The idea had been to use a picture of Clara Bow, the 'it' girl. Somebody blew it. The paper ended up with a picture of Theda Bara. It was weeks before anyone noticed.

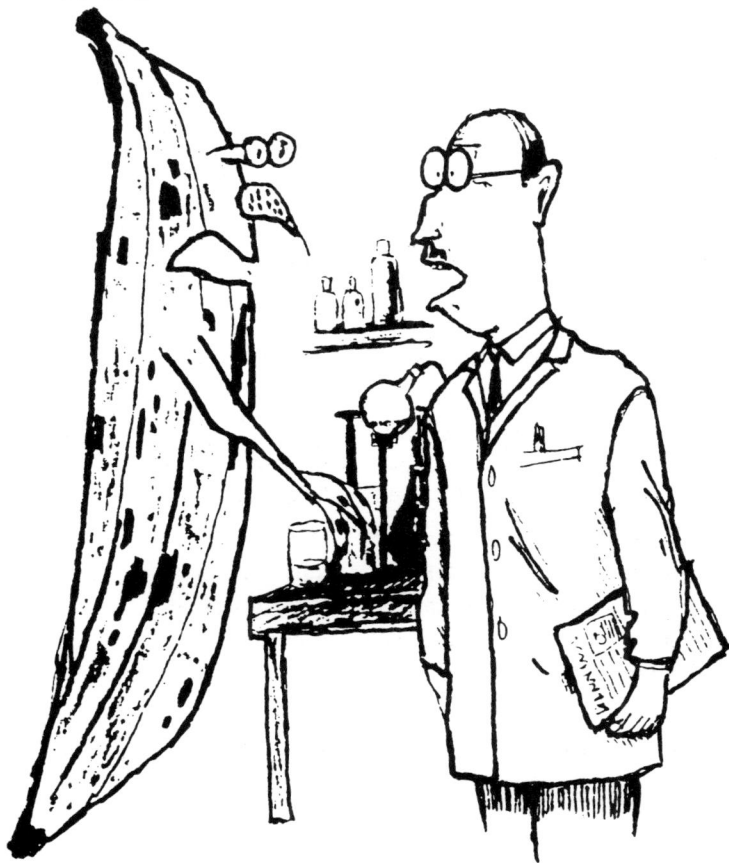

From "Drugs Through The Ages"
Smack In The Eye, Issue 4

From the beginning, the counter-culture of the 'sixties was inspired by the middle classes. John Hopkins, Rosie Boycott, Michael Horovitz, Robin Blackburn, Kieran Fogarty were all university brats. Jagger, Lennon and McCartney all went to grammar school. To working class kids the 'sixties was a dream lying just outside the factory gate. To them it was the first truly accessible dream. To them - unable to play music, paint murals, write poetry - the one sure way in was to take the same drugs.

From the beginning the counter-culture of the 'sixties was underscored by contradictions. Bill Haley's first UK tour took place during the Suez crisis. Thirteen years later, French students (who had provided the Marxist, psychoanalytical framework to the beats' new consciousness) fought running battles with the police on the streets of Paris throughout the 'summer of love' in England and America.

By 1971, all had turned sour. The Beatles had split and John Lennon and Yoko Ono had left for New York. The 'OZ' trial had begun. The English establishment was biting back. All around, the counter-culture was collapsing. In Switzerland, home of Albert Hoffman, Timothy Leary, having escaped gaol in the USA, and a less orthodox 'revolutionary bust' in Algeria at the hands of exiled Black Panther leader, Eldridge Cleaver, was undergoing minor surgery for an ear complaint. Even the guru of the great American LSD dream was tiring of the counter-culture. "Hindu guru groupies", he said, "give me a toothache in my third eye". Weary Leary.

Leary's operation was significant. Throughout the swinging 'sixties, apparently, he had been virtually deaf without the use of a hearing aid; which he was reluctant to contemplate. And if that doesn't add a touch of sweet irony to his oft-quoted slogan; "Turn on. Tune in. Drop out.", then you should stop trying to find *anything* funny. Stay at home and write letters to the local newspapers about rubbish collection. Or get yourself a job as a car park attendant; or with you local authority's equality unit (where you will be able to winge incessantly about the sexism of rubbish collectors). Start a local branch of the Guns 'n' Roses fan club.

Of course the great guru wasn't the only one faking it. Most British drop-outs contrived only to drop so far. There were after all, limits, old chap. When John Lennon arrived at Allen Ginsberg's birthday party to find the great man naked except for a pair of underpants on his head and a sign tied to his dick reading "No waiting" He was shocked to his scouse roots. "You don't do that in front of the birds", he protested to a mutual friend.

But by 1971, even pretence was wearing thin. Jim Morrison, lead singer with the Doors, was found dead in his bath in Paris, by his wife. The cause of death is

Two regular customers take a well-earned breather in the elegant surroundings of the Day-Centre. He was 18, she 14. Sadly, both were to die within 3 years.

shrouded in mystery, but was probably a heroin overdose: the same route out of this life that his wife chose a few years later. Across the world, in America, Sharon Tate, wife of film director Roman Polanski, was found savagely hacked to death in her own house. The perpetrators, it transpired, were a gang of drug-crazed mystics, under the leadership of Charles Manson; a protege of the Beach Boys' Wilson brothers. (Some years later, Polanski rounded on a critic who complained about the amount of blood in a murder scene in one of his films. "Don't tell *me* how much blood can spill out of the human body", he snapped). Drugs weren't fun any more. Drugs were a bloodstain on the carpet. Drugs were a bloated body in the bath.

And so the world shifted course again. And the working class flotsam found itself clinging, bewildered to the wreckage of a ship called 'New World' heading nowhere. By the end of the decade most would have returned to the factories, to the garage workshops in converted railway arches, to the high rise slums. A few would have escaped into a different sort of life. Some would have died.

The day that Big Kenny turned blue was the day I got my first practical lesson in the use of an airway. An airway is a question mark-shaped piece of plastic tubing with a mouthpiece at the end where the full-stop should be. Its use in overdoses is to maintain a clear passage to assist the process of mouth-to-mouth resuscitation. The trick to inserting an airway is to do it quickly and smoothly with a slight upward twist of the wrist just before the far end reaches the back of the throat. This should prevent gagging. A further trick is to cultivate an intractable sinus condition; effectively rendering the first-aider impervious to the smell of fetid breath and vomit. This, too should prevent gagging.

That day had been fairly quiet until the panic began. By the time we raced into the room, Kenny's face had turned the blue-grey colour of a November sky. His hands though, draped across the arms of the chair, were white and bloodless with the veins scored in blue lines across them like the marks in a Stilton cheese. Amongst the babble of voices and the non-stop music from the radio, you could hear the hoarse, barking cough of his breathing. It was the sound that young seals make sometimes when they have been abandoned by their mother.

Eugenie worked quickly and efficiently. The rest of us, I remember, were almost paralysed. The airway proved useless. There were too many obstructions. Big Kenny was a young man built on the old, grand scale. If Isambard Kingdom Brunel had been commissioned to design a man, he'd have made one like Big Kenny. But somehow, we managed to get him turned upside down across the chair. Eugenie knelt down before him and began to excavate the vomit by hand.

She was wearing a bright green sari. The dark stain of mucus and vomit spread from her knees up her thighs as she worked. Never one to miss an opportunity to instruct, she maintained a constant commentary. This, and the coarse corncrake rattle of Big Kenny's occasional desperate breaths, were the only sounds. Nobody spoke. Someone had turned off the radio. Death had crept in. Somewhere in a corner of the room he was waiting. Drumming his fingers. It sounded like the beating of my heart.

Much of the rest went by in silent slow motion. The massaging of the heart. The insertion of the airway. The increasingly clipped and desperate-sounding tone of the commentary. He coughed twice; spluttering, bubbling, watery coughs. His eyes flickered open. Then closed again.

When, at last, his breathing became more regular, someone said, "He can fucking take his gear, Kenny can".

The crisis was past. For then. Life goes on.

Most of our customers were using barbiturates and mandrax, both of which often engendered quite violent behaviour or gross drunkenness and collapse; often within the space of a few minutes. On one occasion I was accosted by a regular attender wielding a bread knife and half a bentwood chair. (The other half had been tested for durability across the head of another regular customer thus hastening the end of the 'pleasantly woozy' stage of *his* mandrax experience!).

"Give me the knife, Pete".

"I'll give it you in the gut, bastard. And him and all".

I sighed heavily as if this really *was* a minor irritation that might have to result in the reluctant use of force, and that I was by no means shitting myself and contemplating a swift dash to the sanctuary of the toilet. (I spent a lot of time, in those days, in contemplation of this kind).

"Give me the knife or I'll break your fucking arm".

"Piss off!".

So much for reality therapy. In the end, and to everyone's surprise, he fell for the proverbial oldest-trick-in-the-book.

"Get back Jim!", I shouted to nobody at all over his shoulder, "he's got a knife".

The glazed eyes turned slowly to peer, with difficulty, behind him. A swift punch in the back; a sickening, crunching stamp on the hand and we were in a position once more to slice our own bread. Minutes later, Pete was sitting as meek as a lamb whilst another worker bathed his badly split lip. The bentwood chair, hurled at the last minute when the ruse had exposed itself, had bounced back off the wall and hit him, quite hard, in the face; probably causing far more damage than I had.

"Sorry man", he mumbled through the lint and sticking plaster, "it's the barbs".

We barred him anyway; and he took it in good part. But sadly, violent incidents of this kind were depressingly - and frighteningly - frequent. Perhaps they could have been handled differently. Certainly, our vigorous and evangelical enforcement of the ideology led, inevitably, to much unnecessary friction. There was a good-sized helping of male ego in there too. Generally the women workers were able to calm these situations better. But all too often the atmosphere was explosive anyway and the return of a barbiturate epidemic remains for me, a personal nightmare.

Some years later, when the barbiturate-devouring hordes from Scotland and the North of England reached the capital city, London day-centres quickly adopted an appointment-based system of service. Of course, there were other, worthier reasons for the sudden change. But the timing and the speed of developments were too much for simple coincidence. For them, the Hun were knocking at the gates of Rome. For us, starting where we had, things could only get better. I seem to remember there was another short-lived craze for platform-soled high-heels around then too. Life goes on.

And both barbiturates and mandrax were frighteningly dangerous to the user too. The risk of accidental overdose was always at hand. Lifeline workers grew to be as skilled - if not more skilled - as casualty nurses in the use of plastic airways. It remains for me, a source of great pride that no-one ever died on the premises; although on a number of occasions we dealt with situations where an attender's heart had actually stopped.

Do these sound like heroic and exciting days? They were not. The violence and death were frightening, grubby and obscene. In 1974, my diary tells me, I attended 27 funerals. I don't remember anyone over twenty-eight and most were far younger.

Two teenage girls, twins, fell from a high-speed train trying to ride between the carriages. They were heading for London to buy Chinese heroin; a substance almost unknown in Manchester. Probably they died instantly and knew very little about it. The autopsy report revealed that both girls had consumed substantial quantities of palfium and mandrax.

Less fortunate was Little Billy, a young man in his late teens. Three weeks out of Borstal and intoxicated with barbiturates, he collapsed over an electric cooker whilst trying to light a cigarette, and lay there unable to move. His burns were horrific; stomach churning. And his tolerance to pain-killing drugs rendered it impossible to properly medicate him. We took turns to sit at his bedside. Eugenie, I remember, was there for almost the whole five days it took for him to die. For me, my short vigil returns occasionally to haunt me still, and remains a crow-black moment of horror in a period filled with despair.

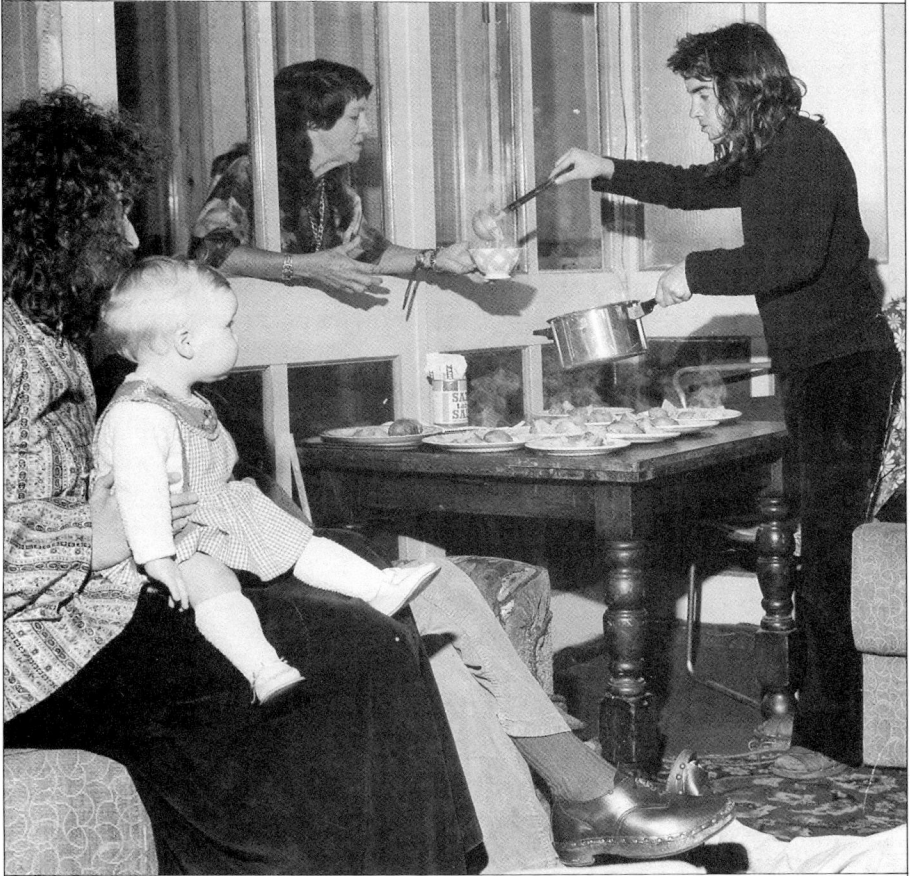

Dinner-time at the Day-Centre. The ubiquitous vegetables in cheese sauce.

Not all the days were so black. Sometimes there really *was* a feeling of comradeship, of care and compassion. The midday meal - a cooked dinner for 35 for a total cost of £6.87 - became a focal attraction which neared ritual and celebration with the Christmas Feast. For Christmas dinner, the planning began weeks before. (So, too, did the begging). Money was raised through collections round pubs. Many of the 'hipper' businesses - On The Eighth Day, Gold Seal, Black Sedan and Seven Miles Out - provided gifts. Usually, the turkeys were too large to be prepared in our small oven and this task was farmed out: twice to the Midland Hotel, once to the police canteen. Only in the first year was the Feast actually held on Christmas Day. In subsequent years, it marked our closure for the holiday period. A blessed relief for us, but a time of desperate loneliness for many of our customers.

For the most part, the line between our spare time and our time at work was blurred. Often we socialised with our customers; often we shared our homes. For two years, some of the workers were accommodated in an empty rectory in Beswick, where a small number of customers could be offered a bed for the night.

There were occasional outings too. For the Bickershaw Festival, workers and customers arrived in droves. On one memorable occasion we descended upon Blackpool for the day. First stop was a pub near the station for a drink and a game of darts. We came close to being ejected when it transpired that Big Dougie had eaten all the chalk. It certainly put paid to the darts. Later came the Funhouse: a small, ragged army of drug users hurtling down the giant slide fortified by 'blobs' (a mixture of Australian white wine and hot water - a useful alternative to mandrax if you can manage to drink enough) served up at Yates' Wine Lodge. One of the party, by then heavily pregnant, had to be almost physically restrained when we hit the big rides; the big dipper, the whirling wheel, the wall of death.

But always the happier events were played out against a backcloth of despair and sudden death. Overdoses, often fatal, were a weekly event. Of the 500 regular attenders during that first year, about half are now dead.

The death and destruction though, had very little impact upon those who remained. Chemist burglaries, the intimidation and deception of doctors and the forgery of prescriptions continued unabated. Prescription forgery led to one of my most embarrassing moments when two regulars - one, a known 'writer' - entered the day-centre, in October, and scuttled down into the basement looking very furtive indeed. I followed with great stealth and was in time to overhear an almost conclusive conversation.

"How do you spell it? Is it 'ie' or 'y'?"

"I don't fucking know. You're the one with the 'O' level!".

That was good enough for me. I marched officiously round the corner and confronted them. "Alright. I know exactly what you two bastards are up to. You know the rules. You can give me the pad and piss off out!".

"No Rowdy. You don't understand. We were just . . ."

"Don't take the piss. I'm not stupid. Just hand it over and get out".

They exchanged exasperated glances, shrugged their shoulders and handed me. . . my birthday card.

"You'd better have this too. It's your birthday present. We were going to nick you some wrapping paper too, but they're a bit hot in Lewis's today".

It was a large illustrated works of Chagall. I felt like dog dirt.

To their credit they found the whole incident immensely amusing and often referred to it; quite fondly and without reproach. I considered at the time whether I should return the book but that seemed, in the circumstances, churlish and prim. Anyway, I thought, Lewis's can stand it. I admit now to pangs of guilt when the store went through a restructuring in the late 'eighties, laying off almost 30% of its work-force. Perhaps . . . But then again, who knows. I am quite sure that mine was not the only straw heaped upon that particular camels back.

But did it pull me up short the next time? Oh no. We had a mission to fulfil. Looking back now, I find it almost physically painful to remember how completely we were hypnotised by our own message. This is not to say that we were wrong. No. Much of what we did then is now regarded as standard practice in modern drug services. (Although on reflection, of course, that probably isn't the same thing at all). Without question, many young people did not die who would have died. Many of our attenders - probably more than now - did stop using. It cannot be said, though, that their lives became as richly fulfiling as we had hoped in return for their sacrifice. Most lives aren't. No, we weren't wrong; just a little naive.

We had little time for simple caring. That, we believed would merely reinforce drug users' victim-focused self-image. People were responsible for their own actions whatever the consequences. Facing up to these realities would inevitably lead to a deeply positive personal catharsis. And so on. And so on.

Oh no. We weren't wrong. We just thought we could make the trains run on time.

CHAPTER THREE

THE DAWN OF MAGIC

" . . . and the therapy wasn't working either.
I even considered committing suicide.
But my analyst is a strict Freudian.
They make you pay for the sessions you miss".

Woody Allen
from
'A Live Performance in New York'

THE DAWN OF MAGIC

Oh yes! Through all of this period, we were held spellbound by our own belief in therapy. It was the answer. And we had it.

I am a good deal older now, though perhaps not that much wiser. Now I find most therapy to be much akin to nuclear power stations. We all know that they have a limited power to achieve their objectives. Many of us suspect that the cost is disproportionate to the outcome. A few of us would like to simply close them down. But then. What would happen to all those unemployed therapists? And what chance for the supply industries which have sprung up around them? Who would buy all those books? Who in their right mind would listen to those turgid, pretentious relaxation tapes? Who among us has not grown, at least *slightly,* tired of the crashing of waves and the endless whooo-whoooing of humpbacked whales?

In the end, perhaps the most sensible thing to do would be to allow a limited continuation with appropriate safeguards for the rest of us. Clearly, therapy should be kept on a leash and securely muzzled when let loose in public: especially around the young and impressionable. Perhaps appropriate labelling with a strict government health warning would help.

It's not that I see no value whatsoever in therapy. No. Many have benefited enormously from it. But then, many have not. Certainly, many therapeutic approaches have reaped dramatic rewards in psychiatry. But increasingly, this is not the field wherein therapy flourishes. More and more, as therapy takes a hold, it is in the private sector. It is as a medium for people who have too much money to spend and very little interesting to say about themselves. From a socialist perspective, this has a kind of perverse irony. As a method for redistributing wealth and preventing bores from pestering you in the bar, therapy may yet prove to be invaluable.

But too often, therapy - in all it's manifestations - has been used to cause further humiliation to those already socially dislocated. To reinforce the therapists power and underline his/her superiority. Perls, the father of Gestalt therapy, boasted in his autobiography of actually physically assaulting a female group member. He had, he told her, 'beaten up more than one bitch' in his life. Carl Jung, it is said, collaborated with the Nazis. Certainly he made little attempt to hide his belief in the inherent superiority of the white races.

Notice anything here? Oh yes, they're all men. So far. The urge to be powerful, to be strong, to be on top - and thus to humiliate - seems to run strong in men. Most of all in men. But there's time yet. And already some early warnings. Melanie Klein thought there was nothing wrong in attempting to psychoanalyse her ten year-old daughter. Just think of that. The analysis was such a stunning success that her daughter subsequently declined to even attend her funeral. In the wake of feminist art and feminist literature has come feminist therapy. (No sign yet of feminist algebra - but don't hold your breath). The damage and distress propagated by therapy thus far, we are assured, is the result of its dominance by men who are dismissed as 'chauvinist' and 'sexist'. Which is a bit like saying that fascism was spoilt by the involvement of the 'krauts' and 'eyeties'. In the Never Never Land of therapy, male therapists are Peter Pans who have never grown up, or Captain Hooks who grew up too fast. Watch out little Wendy! Tinkerbell is on the rampage! You may well end up out of the frying pan and into the fire.

Certainly, since feminist psychotherapy emanates from a section of society (women) who have been traditionally oppressed by the rest (men), it does seem likely that it will offer a refreshing and different perspective. But until therapists - of whatever persuasion or gender - recognise the potential damage which can be inflicted by the instrument they are wielding, danger will lurk behind every tree. In a land where there are no effective gun laws, it is all too easy for the oppressed to become the oppressors.

Therapy came early into the world of the drug user. The invasion was consolidated by the Dangerous Drugs Act of 1968. Based upon the recommendations of the second Brain Committee, the Act took the power to prescribe for addiction, out of the hands of general practitioners (although only in respect of certain drugs such as heroin and cocaine) and relocated it within psychiatry.

In the early years at least, their therapeutic interventions were limited and therefore innocuous. Sadly, embarrassingly, the real 'breakthrough' came from the voluntary sector. Chuck Dederich, a former alcoholic who had been heavily involved in Alcoholics Anonymous in Santa Monica, California, invented the Synanon Game. This led to the formation of the Synanon Community for drug users and proceeded to spawn a proliferation of similar communities across the world. Towards the end of his reign at Synanon, Dederich would lay with new brides in the manner of a medieval squire. At one stage, he ordered all the community's residents to divorce, and remarry other residents of his choice, on a prescribed day. Once, he ordered a rattlesnake to be left in the letterbox of a prosecuting attorney.

These were the historical roots of the therapeutic communities which sprang up around the south of England during the early 1970's. There weren't many. Mostly they mellowed fairly quickly. Mostly they became more 'British'. Mostly, they were established at the instigation of psychiatrists.

The mystery, which still remains, is how such a small number of establishments were able to influence, so dramatically, the developments within the rest of the drug treatment network.

For us, I think, it was the opportunity to share some of the rewards. Some of the power. Like most of the other non-residential services we were poorly resourced; struggling from financial crisis to financial crisis. (It was always easier to finance residential services). Like most of the other services we were working mainly with what would now be called drug users at the 'pre-contemplative stage'. We wanted them to stop using. They wanted to carry on using. To carry on using drugs. And to carry on using the shelter we provided, to use drugs; to talk about drugs; to arrange the acquisition of drugs.

Picture this. We would work with a drug user for years. We would disarm him when he got violent. We would clean up after he had pissed in our broom cupboard. Occasionally, we would be around to administer the airway when he overdosed. And then one day he would get arrested for burglary or something similar. We would plead for him in court. Refer him to a therapeutic community. And if it worked? Then he would send *them* a card every Christmas. (Not us). He would credit *them* with the success of his treatment in any interview with the media. (Not us). How do you think we felt? We wanted some of that power. We wanted some of that kudos. And the key was therapy.

Therapy would deliver us a limited amount of power over our customers. Therapy would enhance our professional standing amongst colleagues from within the National Health Service. Therapy would provide the reward of seeing some customers 'grow' and the justification for excluding those who refused to 'grow'.

We were not alone. Of course. Most of the other drug agencies in England were ploughing a parallel furrow at that time. In 1976, I was the keynote speaker at the annual conference of the Standing Conference of Drug Abuse (SCODA), the co-ordinating body for drugs agencies in the voluntary sector. I had recently returned from a trip to the Netherlands. There, I had been impressed by the adaptation of therapeutic communities to non-residential settings. In my talk I argued that British drug services were, at once too insular and too singular. Mostly they did not look outside their own country for inspiration. When they did, they looked almost exclusively, to America. I argued that there was a wealth of good practice to be observed on the Continent (that was how we talked about Europe then - remember?), and cited a number of examples.

Within a matter of weeks, this lead to the establishment of a Non-Residential Rehabilitation Working Group within SCODA. In the end the Group did little more than redefine existing practice within non-residential drug services. I know, I was an enthusiastic member. It was driven, at least in part, by a desire to right

Surviving In Therapy. From "The Dark Side of The Spoon"
Smack In The Eye, Issue 8

the reward balance between the two ends of the service: where residential services 'did' rehabilitation and 'street agencies' mopped up sick and ladled out soup.

But, above all, therapy was magic. We believed entirely in its mystic power. It marked us out from the others. Perhaps I was more besotted than the rest. At this distance it becomes, sometimes, difficult to focus. But it certainly seems that way to me now.

You should remember. We had to find something. We had renounced the power of the Clinics and their over-medicalising psychiatrists. We knew that was not the way. We knew there had to be *something* better. Hadn't there? But, faced with substantial numbers of drug users who refused to accept responsibility for their actions. Refused to allow themselves to 'grow'. Refused to work upon their low 'self-image'. Who revelled in their drug-taking, their shoplifting and deception, their 'victim role' (with or without the disease model). We felt we had to *do* something.

Some years ago, a Senior Medical Advisor at the Department of Health, remarked that the history of drug treatment policy, in this country, was one of an establishment lurching from one fashionable idea to the next "like a herd of Gaderene swine".

She had a point.

Somewhere in the early 'seventies we lurched into the therapy trap.

In 1972, after prolonged discussion, we decided to provide a two-tier day centre. Those who were drug-free that day, could partake of all that we had to offer - candle and enamel brooch making, the free midday meal, discussion groups, music classes. Those who were intoxicated would be restricted to the two ground-floor reception rooms.

It didn't work. It was illogical and unfair. Those who had used barbiturates, (which caused exaggerated and obvious drunkenness), were inevitably restricted. Those who had used opiates (which didn't), were allowed a free run of the facilities. We were forced to amend the rule to read that the division would be between those who appeared - *to us* - capable of spending the day without enamelling themselves during brooch making, falling asleep during discussion groups, falling into their free midday meal; and those who did not appear - *to us* - to be so capable. The rule thus lurched from the objective to the subjective. Suddenly, the decision lay within our discretion. Inevitably, its administration became inconsistent. Inevitably, it became a source of friction between ourselves and our customers.

I don't think that there's anything necessarily wrong with friction. Actually, I think it's got rather a lot going for it. But I do think it's wrong for any agency to dissipate its energy in fruitless, endless, going-nowhere arguments.

But, in some form or other, we stuck with this division of our customers throughout most of that decade. It was the bedrock upon which most of our therapeutic aspirations were founded. We needed to sort the sheep from the goats. The intoxicated from the drug free. The unmotivated from the motivated. Only those who were motivated to change could really benefit from the therapeutic tools at our disposal.

And we built up our stock of therapeutic tools as assiduously as the Water Rat piled up those heaps of small arms and cudgels for Toad and Badger and Mole. (Here's a gestalt for the Mole. Here's a gestalt for the Badger. Here's a gestalt for the Toad. Here's a psychodrama for the Mole. Here's a psychodrama for the Badger. Here's a psychodrama for the Toad . . . .). We undertook courses in gestalt (yes!), and dramatherapy, and transactional analysis and counselling (the poor man's therapy), and a hundred more.

Of course, half of the time, what we did was not therapy at all. Half of the time it was simply about the management of our resources. About creating order out of chaos. But we were the alternative society. Rules were for 'straights'. We had no desire to be seen as day-centre policemen. So we applied to our rules a veneer of therapy. Camouflaged them with the notion of personal growth.

Everything became a therapeutic exercise. Everything had a personal growth pay-off. Some mornings I would read aloud, snippets from the newspaper to encourage discussion. One morning I read that a hospital in London, whose streets were, even then, silting up with traffic, had reinstituted their pigeon cote and were using carrier pigeons to take blood samples to a laboratory across the city.

"Well, what did they do with them before?", someone asked.

I consulted the newspaper again.

"It says here that they used to put them in taxis".

"But", said one of our less personally grown customers, "didn't they shit on the seats?"

And all the time our numbers dropped. And all the time those who weren't 'motivated' found better places to go. Until we became something we had never intended to be. An agency designed almost exclusively for those committed to change. An agency with little to offer those who were using drugs and could see no reason to change; or at least no possibility of attaining the standards we had set for them.

Somewhere in there, I expelled a young woman for refusing to talk to an empty chair. Somewhere in there, a researcher discovered a drug user who had chosen to do a three-year prison sentence rather than seek a referral to Lifeline, because "they do your head in; make you talk to chairs and things". Just think of that.

Somewhere in there, we had decided that forming meaningful relationships with furniture was more important than preventing drug users from going to prison.

And the process continued relentlessly. We established written contracts. Work penalties. We encouraged customers to draw life-maps. To confront themselves. To talk to chairs.

Not all of this was bad. We were learning much about drug users. (Particularly about their resilience). We were changing peoples beliefs about drug use, about drug users and their capacity to change.

We established a bail assessment service and, thus, were the first drugs agency to offer a specific service, other than legal advice and representation, to drug users in the criminal justice system. We appointed the first training officer post in the drugs field. We experimented with detached work. We ran abstinence groups in prisons.

But almost all of our work was interlaced with therapeutic notions. It gnawed away at everything we did. And, although sometimes the end result was much better than the original conception, it became the starting point for most of our thinking.

For the majority of our customers, their problems were those of homelessness, unemployment, poverty, illiteracy, loneliness. But we wanted to see more. We wanted to dig down to the personal growth bedrock. For us, there could be no half measures. Thinking back, it seems as if it had never occurred to us that it can be hard to 'grow' when you can't read and write and you don't know where you're going to sleep that night. We didn't ignore these material issues, but our therapeutic disease belittled and mocked them. I cherish now a research article from 'Psychology Today' which showed that letting out (or 'getting in touch with') your anger can be very bad for you. It was certainly very bad for us.

Some, perhaps many, of our customers could have benefited from therapeutic approaches in a safe environment. Our great folly was in believing that we had created one. Many had been sexually, or physically, abused. Little Billy had been regularly beaten by his alcoholic father. Sheila had been locked in a cupboard under the stairs for three days for 'stealing' bread from the kitchen table. Maggie Singh, born in a tenement in Dundee, was repeatedly sexually abused by an 'uncle' in front of her mother. She was taken into care and placed in a convent-run orphanage. She arrived late at night and was unceremoniously deloused and sent to bed. In the morning, when it was discovered that she had wet the bed, one of the nuns tied the sheet around her neck and sent her down to breakfast to meet her new friends. Later she was to agree to a marriage of convenience with an Iranian student. When he discovered her drug problem, he decided to make it a real marriage and 'save' her. But he too, it seems, beat and abused her.

Backgrounds of this kind were not uncommon, and drugs provided a way of dulling the pain. Therapy may have helped, but the over-riding need for the Little Billys, the Sheilas and the Maggies was to find a place of safety; to escape from the crushing round of prison, homelessness and despair. Personal restructuring could wait.

In the end, it was the dramatic escalation in drug use at the end of the seventies which tore us out of the therapy trap.

The standard theory now, is that as drug use grew at the end of the 'seventies, it began to encompass the lives of young people whose lives were, otherwise, quite normal. The new drug users were ordinary working class youths whose unemployment, criminal activity, anti-social behaviour was a result of (rather than a precursor to) their drug use. That's the theory.

But how much do we know? In truth we have no real facts to base this theory upon. We have no idea how many of our customers in the early 'seventies started committing crimes before they started using drugs. Unemployment rose at the end of the 'seventies, and throughout the 'eighties, at approximately the same rate as the growth of known drug use. The poverty pool got bigger. We argue that the drug users of the 'eighties had much more in common with their non-drug using counterparts. But we know very little about the relationship between drug users in the early 'seventies and *their* non-drug using counterparts. Nobody ever bothered to find out. Many theorists have characterised them as having 'Bohemian lifestyles'. Somehow I've always thought that Bohemianism might be more attractive than that. And what of these new drug users? What of the "street-wise runts of the 'eighties?" Are the drug users of the 'eighties *really* any less emotionally scarred than their counterparts in the 'sixties and 'seventies? Any less anti-social? Criminal? Any less unemployed? All we really do know, is that the number of known drug users got bigger. Much bigger.

All we really know, is that with drug use so dramatically increased. So obviously present upon our streets. It was no longer good enough to simply confine the majority of our work to those who could jump through the requisite number of therapeutic hoops.

Whatever the validity of the theory, it succeeded in changing the face of drug services for ever.

For me the change was devastating. I had spent the past ten years learning therapeutic techniques. Introducing myself to cushions. Breaking up into small

Biting Back in Therapy
From "The Dark Side of The Spoon"
Smack In The Eye, Issue 8

groups to share my experience. Hugging other social workers. And nurses. And drama teachers. And youth workers. Thanking them for sharing with me. Sharing with them (though only a little). Talking to chairs.

Suddenly. Inexplicably. The world had been turned upside down. Much of what I had believed in, was slipping away. Had already slipped away. It wasn't like waking up. It was much more like falling down. Slowly. Ask any former believer in Transcendental Meditation at what point they came to believe that yogic flying was merely bouncing up and down. On a mattress. With your legs crossed. They can't tell you. It was so gradual. Sometimes the ground you stand upon. Or believe you stand upon. Becomes worn away. Other realities grow up through it. Like trees. Until there are so many trees that you can't see the horizon anymore. You just have to turn around and look in another direction if you want to see the sky. To register the horizon. It was a lot like that. Slow, imperceptible at first. And then, all in a rush, so that there didn't seem any other direction your thoughts could lead you.

And yet.

This dramatic change, was in some ways - for me at least - almost reassuring. It represented a return to the simple, the pragmatic, the practical. Once again I was to become the organisation's handyman. Just like I was in those early months. Throughout those early months, I had talked to the customers. Between jobs. Sometimes during them. During coffee breaks. I had been stunned to hear that the Management Committee, when a vacancy occurred, had been assured that my counselling skills were 'exceptional'. I hadn't really been sure what counselling actually was. Now, after a decade of striving to understand the complexities of counselling and the higher arts of therapy, I was returning to the notion that just talking to people. Letting them talk. Offering advice and practical help was not in the least mundane. No. It was what we should all have been striving for in the first place. Oh! delicious irony.

It was not that our therapeutic endeavours were wrong. It is quite clear that many drug users really are emotionally scarred. That therapeutic techniques, applied judiciously and eclectically can provide a powerful remedy. What was wrong was the assumption that all drug users were like this during the 'seventies. What was also wrong was the assumption that, after 1980, all drug users were not.

I would not want you to think that I entirely dismiss the work we were able to do. I remain immensely proud of our achievements during that period. We achieved a great deal that was of value to drug users. And we did it against the odds. For most of the seventies we employed only three staff. Never, until after 1979 was the staff team more than five. Often we literally ran out of money. We always survived. But only because of the commitment of the staff and volunteers.

The possibility that some of that commitment may, in retrospect, have been misdirected does not, I believe, diminish the stature of the achievement.

But like many others at that time, we were firing all our bullets at one target. That was a mistake.

Somewhere between the pragmatic and the esoteric lies something that, just about, looks like the truth. Perhaps it has to do with age. I would never have accepted such a premise as a young man. But then. Life is, after all, a little like an old bed. The longer you use it for lying in, the more you find that there is a tendency to roll towards the middle.

CHAPTER FOUR

THE BODY POLITIC

"Politics is pig shit!"

Richard Neville
from
'OZ' Magazine

THE BODY POLITIC

Throughout the early years, the shape of the Lifeline Project resembled what organisational analysts have called a 'power culture'.

The Project was founded by, and built around, the remarkable Dr. Eugenie Cheesmond. I have rarely, in my life, encountered such a combination of determination, vision, stubbornness and energy. I have heard people say that starting a voluntary project in the drugs field these days is well nigh impossible. What with contract culture, they say. And outcome measures, they say. And business plans, they say. All I would say to *them* is this. Try 1971!

It is not a delusion created by distance that the establishment of Lifeline Project was difficult and painful. Drug use has always been unpopular. It was never possible - as with some more cuddly charities - to place fibreglass models of drug users, with slots in the top of their heads, outside Sainsbury's and wait for the money to roll in. The Project was always going to be shackled to public sector grant aid. But back then, the public sector was far more reluctant to recognise the need for such expenditure. Even when the Project was opened and seeing sixty to eighty drug users a day, the initial response of Manchester City Council was to claim that there was no significant drug problem in the City. To their credit, they reversed that decision within the first year and have remained major funders ever since.

A Regional Drug Dependence Unit had been established at Prestwich Hospital, in response to central government entreaties, in the late 'sixties. For the first five years, until the reorganisation of the Health Service in 1974, the costs were provided centrally. They couldn't have been very much. The Unit consisted of a part-time Medical Superintendent who had been due for retirement. Salford Social Services seconded a social worker and nursing cover was provided by the outpatient sister; in addition to her other duties.

By the middle of the 'seventies, the Unit could muster a role-call of twenty-seven drug users. Theoretically, the Unit had been established to provide a service for the whole of Greater Manchester and Lancashire; but in practice it saw few people outside its immediate catchment area. Most of those registered with the new Unit, received maintenance prescriptions for heroin (and later, physeptone; an early, injectable form of methadone): a few also received cocaine. The Unit experimented with a variety of different treatments including the infamous sleep treatment and electro-convulsive therapy: but with no great success. It probably didn't matter that much; the Unit saw their work anyway, as a kind of holding exercise. Orthodox opinion at that time was that there was no real treatment for addiction and that the best that could be done was to "contain the whirlwind of destruction" which it caused to others.

Notice anything familiar?

There was no contact between the Unit and the Lifeline Project; despite our repeated efforts. Staff were instructed by the Medical Superintendent not to speak to us. Patients were warned that their prescriptions would be stopped if they were found to have visited our premises. (Many *did* visit despite these threats). To the staff of the Unit, it seems, we were dangerous, wild-eyed radicals who probably used drugs ourselves; or sold drugs; or slept with drug users; or sacrificed goats at full-moon. Our employment of former drug-users as volunteers and even paid staff only deepened the mistrust and antipathy. Certainly, no Health Service funding would be forthcoming for many years.

But these early difficulties, by emphasising the outlaw, outcast nature of the venture, actually served to strengthen the power culture which Eugenie had created. Volunteers and paid staff were all equally involved in the scrabble for finance. The fact that it was unpopular merely underlined our evangelism. More. It made us feel separate from the rest of the voluntary sector. The voluntary sector, we saw as a range of, usually, fairly acceptable charities, involved in the business of providing sticking plaster for those who fell through the gaps in statutory provision. We were engaged, we believed, in a venture far more fundamental than that. *We* were intent, in partnership with our drug using customers, on creating an alternative and parallel society.

So the normal procedures and established business practices were not for us. Many good and kind volunteers to our Management Committee left exasperated after one or two meetings; frustrated and outraged by our unwillingness to play the game by the rules. I remember gaining an audience with one potential funder by camping outside his door for three days. Needless to say, we had not bothered to submit a formally costed proposal.

I remember reading somewhere, that Chuck Dederich, the founder of Synanon, was asked by the New York Probation Department, how to establish a similar community in New York. His advice, apparently, was that they should give him so many thousand dollars and not "fuck him around" asking for receipts and such like. We had a lot of time for the Dederich approach in those days.

It has to be said. Our methods of doing business then won us few friends. Often, we recruited life-long enemies to our cause. Somebody used to tell a story about two psychologists on holiday in rural France. Hearing of a local farmer who had managed to train his donkey to perform quite unbelievable feats, they determined to go and see for themselves. Being psychologists, they were less interested in the performance than the method. How had he done it, they asked. "Oh", the farmer replied, "just a lot of patience and a great deal of client-centred counselling". Enthralled, they asked for a demonstration; at which the farmer

The Author in 1977. All geared up for contract culture. Note the 'Paddy's Irish Whiskey' sweatshirt; an early form of sponsorship.

took up his stick and dealt the donkey a shuddering blow between the eyes. "But that's not client-centred counselling", they screamed. "Oh no", the farmer responded, "that's just to get his attention". Our approach to fund-raising, not to mention many other areas of our work, certainly had some similarities.

The spell was broken, for me, in 1975. By the late Autumn it had become clear that not only was there barely enough money to survive the financial year, but there was almost no promise of funding for the next. It was agreed that we should ask the National Association for the Care and Resettlement of Offenders (NACRO) to examine the possibility of a rescue package. What happened next, is still a painful and difficult mystery for me to unravel.

Eugenie had been increasingly spending most of her time out of the Project at a residential centre we were hoping to open. The burden of running the day centre had therefore fallen upon the rest of the team. Both Eugenie and I had spoken of giving up our work with the Project. Eugenie had talked, at length, of her plans to return to South Africa. When NACRO reported back, the news was all bad. The residential centre could not survive. The day centre could, but there would need to be at least one redundancy. Since they understood that Dr. Cheesmond was planning to return to South Africa . . . . My stomach turned. I remember feeling physically sick. Could the day-centre function with just three staff? I was asked. I heard myself say yes. I knew it was a knife in the back. The spell was shattered.

Oh, we tried to rebuild it. The following day, during a day-long discussion. We assured Eugenie that if her plans to leave had not been fixed, then we would go back to the Committee and insist that we had been wrong; that the day centre could *not* be run by three people. Or we would insist that they made one of us redundant instead. It wasn't any good. The dream had vanished. Eugenie's departure from the Project she had built was now inevitable and, when it came, painful both for her, and for me.

Our incorporation into NACRO was painful too. We were their only drug project and the only established agency they had ever taken over. It would be a long way from the truth to suggest (as we thought then) that NACRO was overly bureaucratic. But it was a well-established national charity and we had never experienced this kind of organisational structure before.

Within days, we began to receive memoranda. I had never seen anything like them before. Amongst one of the earliest clutches, I remember, was an invitation to take part in a staff raffle for invitations to the Queen's Garden Party. Since the Queen was NACRO's patron, they were allowed to send two staff members a year to the event. For renegade drug workers, this was almost too much.

I suppose we were truculent. I'm sure that for my part, I was rude, and probably childish. We quarrelled from the beginning. NACRO wanted me to be the Project Leader. We insisted that we should run as a workers collective. We lost. So we established a salary pool instead.

Within six months I found myself embroiled within NACRO's disciplinary procedure and facing immediate dismissal. For NACRO, this was almost certainly a tactical error. For me it was a thunderbolt. When I received the letter, I cried for the first time since my teens. At least, for the first time without alcohol, or other drugs to lubricate the tear ducts and drop stones into the well of self pity.

From then on, I suppose, it was for me, a kind of a war. Oh, there were occasional truces; cease-fires to allow the opportunity to bury our respective slain. But the battle lines were drawn with indelible pencil.

And as much as anything, it was probably my embittered hostility to management that obscured from me the dreadful damage that political involvement was beginning to sow within the Project. It was not until we, once again, became independent, that we began to reap the harvest of that development; and that was not until 1983.

Richard Neville, the sometime-editor of OZ Magazine had coined the expression "Politics is pig shit!" in the 'sixties. In many ways, this defined our political position as an organisation.

It was not that we weren't interested or involved in politics as individuals. We were. But, as an organisation, we saw politics as another cynical facet of 'straight' society. The politics of the left seemed closer to our aspirations. But even here, our interests diverged. The left had set it's sights on the overthrow of the state. *We* simply wanted to walk away from the state and create something better. At one stage, in the early 'seventies, we attempted to buy an abandoned village in Wales. We were going to step outside society and create a new order. But we hoped that the old order would keep sending the unemployment benefits.

There had always been this uneasy alliance between the left and the counter-culture of the 'sixties. In the early days it was underlined by CND and the Aldermaston Marches. Later there was the campaign against the war in Vietnam. Mick Jagger and Horace Ove hurling stones at the police in Grosvenor Square. Michael de Freitas (later Michael Abdul Malik, then Michael X) was a contributor to 'International Times' (IT). The first women's edition of 'Frendz' was compiled by women from the Angry Brigade; though no-one knew it at the time. But this was the spark that lit the fuse that exploded as 'Spare Rib' magazine in 1972. (It also reduced part of the official residence of Home Secretary, Robert Carr, to rubble).

So in many ways, the Project had always been a political entity. In my early teens, I had been a member of the Young Communist League. During the seventies, I rejoined the Communist Party of Great Britain. Many of us - paid staff and volunteers - were subscribers to CND, Anti-Apartheid, Chile Solidarity Campaign. Some were members of the Labour Party: some, of other left splinter groups. Our customers accompanied us on demonstrations in support of the Shrewsbury Two, the Anti-Nazi League, the Grunwick Pickets. But as an organisation, our alignment with the left was merely coincidental. Socialism was attractive because it appeared to offer justice and fairness and parity. In reality, the 'politics' of the Project were the politics of the alternative; not the underclass.

In 1966, Andrew Oldham - then producer/manager of the Rolling Stones - bought advertising space in 'New Musical Express' entreating the nation's youth to buy copies of the Mamas and Papas' new single; 'California Dreaming', instead of voting in the forthcoming general election; "which can only bring more bigotry, unfulfilled promises and the ultimately big bring-down". Politics was pig shit.

Before the mass evacuation of St. Kilda in the thirties, the islanders had regularly met in the only street to decide the days work. It was dubbed, by mainlanders, the 'St. Kilda Parliament'. I suppose, in many ways, the politics of our organisational structure retained a great deal of the St. Kilda Parliament. Ours was an old-fashioned anarchy rather than any allegiance to a formal political creed.

But gradually, the hard, tight-lipped face of political dogma, began to haunt our every meeting. Our traditional use of volunteers was eschewed, since it was believed to threaten the security of the paid workforce. "If a job was worth doing it was worth being paid for". Therapy had erected the barricades between ourselves and our customers. Politics performed a similar function in respect of a whole community who wished to contribute to our work.

And yet the day had begun so well. In the early 'eighties, we became once more independent. We were eager to embark upon a socialist experiment in management. Within five years, we found ourselves in the middle of the drug field's first strike.

How we got there, I am still at a loss to explain. The arguments became increasingly bitter. Increasingly personal. Increasingly painful. On one occasion, after an extremely heated dispute, I was accused of threatening physical violence to a staff member. I hadn't. But the option was not without its attractions; certainly in terms of the short-term, immediate rewards.

One night, I dreamt that I had bought a pick-axe handle and put it in the boot of my car. On arriving at work, I had invited one of my most prominent antagonists into the car park to look at it. Any more of your crap, I told him, and

41

you'll get this across you legs. When I woke in the morning to find that I still considered the idea a serious possibility, I knew that things were coming to a head.

Eventually, towards the end of an extremely protracted disciplinary procedure (which had been accompanied by a strike), it occurred to me that, perhaps, enough was indeed enough. I had been reading John Harvey Jones' autobiography, dealing with his days as head of ICI. "There were times", he pronounced, "when I wondered what a merchant seaman was doing running the worlds biggest pharmaceutical company".

For myself, I began to wonder too.

By then, it had begun to feel as if there was no-one left in the organisation I could fully rely upon. As Brutus said to Caesar, (or might have done), "We just want you to know that me and the lads are right behind you, governor". It seemed it was time to go.

Again, it was a time for tears. I wrote a long, and painful, letter of resignation.

Shortly before the battle of Waterloo, the English succeeded in bribing Blucher, who agreed to change sides. When all seemed as if it might be lost, and the French might be the victor, Blucher led the Prussians in; against Napoleon. For Napoleon, it was the point when everything turned against him. From that moment, he was doomed to a long holiday, in what might well be the worlds least attractive seaside resort (if you exclude Workington and Ardrossan).

For me too, the wind changed at that moment; though for me, it blew in a different direction. I was asked to return as Acting Director by the Management Committee. A number of staff appeared on my doorstep, or telephoned to confirm their support. Two groups of staff wrote to the Management Committee, demanding that I be asked to return. I returned.

But things would never be the same again. Much of what I had believed in had been destroyed by that period. Lifeline Project entered a period of bureaucracy which would have been inconceivable at its inception. I left the Communist Party and joined the Labour Party. I'd had enough of socialism.

In the ensuing months, a number of people left the organisation. My emotions were mixed: many had been my colleagues, for a number of years. Gradually, management became a thing that actually happened, rather than just something we told the funders we did.

In the meantime, the Project had begun to flourish, despite the internal battles. In 1979, joint work on a development plan between Lifeline, NACRO and SCODA resulted in a successful bid for funding. The staff team tripled. In spite of ourselves we had learned a great deal from NACRO; about organisation, about

OUT FROM THE SHADOWS

LIFELINE PROJECT
10th Anniversary Report
by Rowdy Yates

The Tenth Anniversary Report. Written entirely in a gorilla suit, the report has become a collectors item in many Psychiatric Out-patient Departments.

budgeting and structuring funding applications. What's more, the Regional Drug Dependence Unit had taken down the crucifixes and bunches of garlic from their front door. A new consultant had arrived and actually visited the Project to talk about the possibility of some joint-working. It was to be the beginning of a partnership which delivered to the North West a network of drug treatment services which remains the envy of much of the rest of the country.

The world outside was changing too. Drug use had become a high-profile political issue. When in December 1982, the Government's own Advisory Council on the Misuse of Drugs published their report 'Treatment and Rehabilitation', the Department of Health responded by immediately announcing a substantial central fund to 'pump-prime' new drug treatment initiatives.

The Lifeline Project began to grow rapidly. Too rapidly. And, for all of us, the growing pains were almost unbearable.

By the middle of the 'eighties, we were already one of the largest drug projects in the country; with a team of fieldworkers seconded to Community Drug Teams across Greater Manchester and a large and well-respected training unit.

Outside the organisation, things had begun to change dramatically too. Every health authority district in Greater Manchester and Lancashire had established a Community Drug Team. Many of these Teams included Lifeline workers. For the first time since the establishment of England's therapeutic communities in the 'sixties, there was a bridgehead between the National Health Service and the voluntary sector drugs field. And it happened in the North West. Not only that, but many of these new services looked to agencies, such as Lifeline, to lead the way. To establish the ground rules.

But how did we get there? We hid our outlaw masks and signed on as deputies in a new posse. We took every plum we could reach and stuffed it into our mouths whole; with both hands. We thought that we could sort out the ideology later. We traded in our kaftans and we hustled.

In some ways, the need to hustle in the 'eighties, after the need to struggle in the 'seventies, came as almost second nature. When, in 1981 we wanted to celebrate our tenth anniversary, by luring an appropriate celebrity to open our new day-centre in Joddrell Street, we discovered that Eleanor Bron was performing at a theatre in the city.

Perfect.

I spent days phoning some obscure agency in London trying to secure her services. Getting nowhere. Eventually, exasperated, I demanded to know who I was speaking to.

"Oh I'm Sebastian So-hyphen-So. I'm Ms. Bron's agent and I'm in constant contact with her. I'll make sure your request is put to her. Although, of course, she is very busy . . . ."

Good enough.

It was the work of a few minutes to ring the local theatre and announce myself in my new persona.

"I'm sorry, Ms. Bron's in a dress rehearsal and she simply cannot be disturbed".

"Oh, I understand entirely, but I'm Sebastian So-hyphen-So, and I absolutely must speak to her immediately on a matter of the greatest urgency.

And when the great lady was brought to the phone. Oh, then came the real hustle-task.

"Now you're either going to find this endearingly cheeky or your going to swear and hang up. You see, I'm not really Sebastian So-hyphen-So. I'm Rowdy Yates and our organisation, which you may have heard of . . . .".

She didn't laugh. But she came. I wrote her a nice little speech about how a society is judged by it's capacity to care for those less able to care for themselves. How the stature of those at the top of the ladder is ultimately measured against their compassion for those at the bottom; struggling for a foothold. And so on. And so on. She didn't use any of it. But the press had had it quoted in the press releases; so they used it anyway.

A similar line on humanity and compassion was used by the Labour Party during the 1992 general election. Society voted in droves for greed and selfishness.

And how else did we celebrate our tenth birthday? How else! We hosted a 'sixties disco. I spent the whole night sweating inside a gorilla suit. Gorillas made only a marginal contribution to the 'sixties counter-culture revolution. But that, in combination with a number of other seriously crazy events that evening, echoed the lunacy of the 'happenings' organised during the 'sixties by Jeff Nuttall, Michael Horovitz, Spike Hawkins and others. The highlight of the evening came when two sixteen year-old girls won the best 'sixties costume competition. They were into the 'sixties in a big way. But they'd happened upon the disco by chance. It seems they always dressed that way. They received their prize in bemused silence, made their apologies and left. (But not before they had disclosed to a gorilla on the door, that this had been one of the best nights of their lives). Just think of that. Life goes on.

It was the emergence of AIDS in the middle of the 'eighties which allowed us to hone up the edge of our increasingly blunted sword. AIDS was the new plague. Drug users were a high-risk group; along with homosexuals and black immigrants. Communists weren't; but in all other respects, AIDS could have

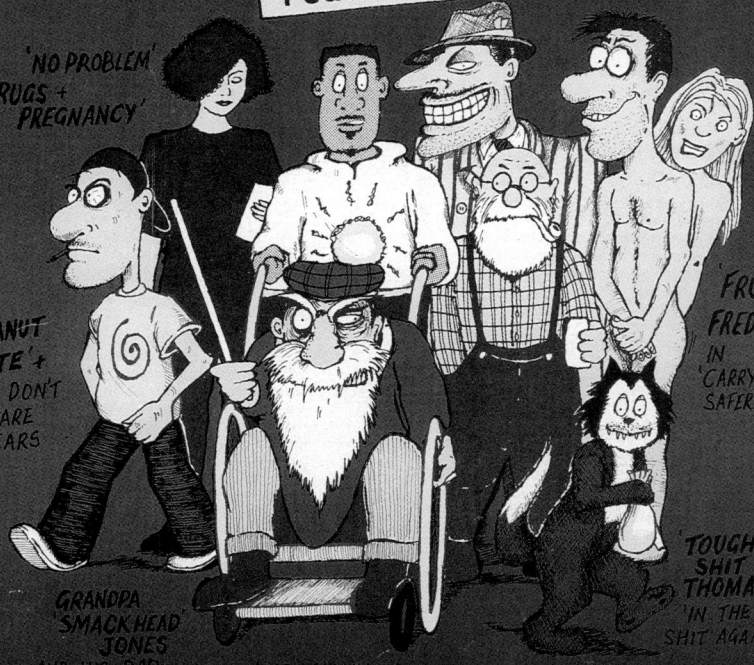

"'Smack In The Eye' was not just a Comic"

been crafted by the CIA. Almost overnight, drug users became not only distasteful, but something much more. Drug users became *really dangerous*. They were potential carriers of a killer disease. Needle-sharing was to be discouraged, prevented, *at all costs*. Drug services were to be given virtual carte-blanche. It was even acceptable to admit, that some of your customers did not strive towards abstinence.

AIDS was the exercise bicycle we jumped on just in time. And we pedalled like mad to get rid of that unsightly flab. We published a widely-read policy document. We established the regions first formal needle exchange. And then, something else happened. We found ourselves in the comic business.

Looking back, I can't really remember why we did it. It may have been that we had 'vision'. It may have been that we had the bottle; and no-one else dared. It may have been simply that we were aching for a little fun; that we wanted to kick a few cans around. Whatever it was, 'Smack in the Eye', was not just a comic. It was the point at which our trajectory, and that of our colleagues in the Health Service, once more parted company. And the further away we got, the harder we pedalled.

And the comic brought in a result which we had hardly dared hope for. Somehow, without really expecting it, our fumbling fingers had dialled a forgotten number. Somewhere in a dusty office, painted emperor purple and pink, a long-silent telephone jangled. A group of rather shabby hippies were shaken out of a *really, really* serious reverie. They looked at each other in surprise. There was a long pause, and then one of them gingerly picked up the handset.

"Hello, early 'seventies here. Furry Freak Brothers speaking".

Suddenly, we found we had re-opened the line of communication. And it worked in both directions. Drug users began to write in to the comic with tips, with complaints, even with suggestions for future stories. Incredibly, it seems, we'd found our way back. And it made dealing with the outrage - and there was a lot of that too - so much easier. Oh yes, we would say, but we've got the only harm reduction literature in the country which receives fan mail. When Pink Floyd played at Maine Road, samisdat photocopies of 'Smack in the Eye: Issue One' were on sale up and down the queues. Breach of copyright had never been so welcome.

The publication of the comic was fraught with difficulties. Many - including many professionals in the drug field - found it outrageous and disgusting. One letter from a tranquilliser helpline informed us that we were "degenerate scum". One member of the Advisory Council on the Misuse of Drugs made a formal complaint to the police. I received two visits from the police as a result. On the second occasion, two officers informed me that they were considering prosecuting me under the Obscene Publications Act. I replied that I would be overjoyed to test the publication in the courts and they departed somewhat bemused. This was not an act of bravery on my part. I was so convinced of the virtue of the comic that I could not conceive that I would ever be convicted. On reflection now, I am not so sure that my confidence was so well placed. However, no prosecution was ever brought although there continue to be occasional angry mutterings.

What was probably more significant, was the changes that the comic engendered; both within the organisation and without. Within the organisation the comic became a focus for our belief that the Lifeline Project could, and should, be visibly, tangibly different to similar NHS services. The comic was also pivotal in altering the views which drug users themselves held of the organisation. We began to be seen as an organisation that was 'on their side'. Just as we had been in the beginning.

But more than anything, 'Smack in the Eye' provided graphic proof of the dangerous and rocky terrain we would find ourselves travelling through in our return to a more radical approach. For a brief period, we had found ourselves the honoured guest at the party. We had, fleetingly, even been invited to be seated at the head of the table. Now, we were to return to our former station; outside in the snow. Stamping our feet to ward off the cold: our noses pressed up against the window.

From this point onward, we would be required to play a very tricky game. For our customers, we would need to build upon a reaffirmed identity which marked us out from the other services with which they might come into contact. For our funders and our colleagues in the field, we would need to provide, painstakingly, absolute proof that, whilst what we were doing was different, it was nonetheless both valid and valuable.

The problem now, was to look both ways without seeming two-faced. Like comic book heroes, we became masters of a thousand disguises. We were the aging hippy mystics on the Nirvana trail. Peering from beneath grizzled brows, we could just make out the faint imprint of where the path had once been. We were the crafty pirates, digging up chest-fulls of treasure before anyone knew there was a map. We were the city-slickers from 'back East'. We knew all about contracts and business plans, and service specifications. 'And if you don't give us the deeds to your ranch we'll tie you to the railroad track'. We were the sweet voices of reason. We could run the commentary on a coronation better than Richard Dimbleby. We were the mad scientists, gibbering over our bubbling, steaming apparatus, awaiting, with maniacal glee the necessary lightening.

It wasn't a game designed to make us very popular with other agencies in the field. We had been intimately involved in the establishment of many of the new

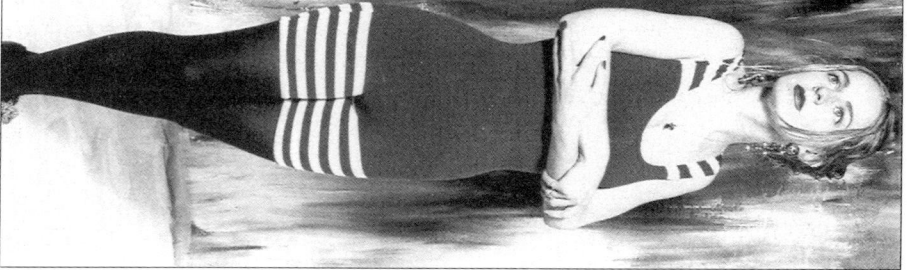

The end of the 'Eighties brought an increasing need to market our services as imaginatively as possible. Shown here are two examples of this strategy: one published in the 91/92 Manchester United Fixture List, the other, a flyer-style Information Leaflet, designed for (and by) young women and distributed at raves.

drug services which had sprung up in the 'eighties in North-West England. They had taken shape, in many cases, in response to our advice. And now, we were changing tack once more. Denying evidence which had our fingerprints all over it. We didn't leave everything behind us. We were carrying some pretty important baggage. But, like fugitives, expecting at any minute to go down in a hail of bullets, we kept on the move and we spread out.

This was not simply the competitive urge. This was survival. By 1989, it was clear to every health authority in the country that they were expected to have established a community-based drug service. Normally, it was assumed that this would be a multi-disciplinary service, drawing, in the main, from the medical, nursing and social work professions. Furthermore, all health authorities had been instructed that they had to establish a district drugs advisory committee. But there was no onus, upon *any* agency or authority, to provide an additional service such as we had come to represent. Our best hope was clearly to continue to offer new, hopefully exciting and innovative, approaches. But this means maintaining a very volatile organisation, a goal which sits uneasily with the increasing need, within contract culture, to be more business-like; more saleable; to offer a more consistent 'product' which can be measured for quality; like apprentices used to be measured for a Montagu Burton suit.

How long we can maintain the momentum? I simply don't know. The contract culture spawned by the Thatcher revolution has already begun to bite. Dramatic changes are taking place against a background of public services decimated by cash shortages. In such circumstances, a loyal opposition (or, perhaps, a rogue elephant) may come, increasingly, to be seen as an unaffordable luxury.

CHAPTER FIVE

DREAM DANCING

"At that moment, too, heaven ran red, a stormy-ribbed blood red. The fierce colour was reflected on the water, and watching eyes grew dazed, not so much by light as by instinctive fear. From cloud to cloud rolled this red thunder of daybreak."

Neil M. Gunn
from
'Morning Tide'

DREAM DANCING

A little before daylight, on 15th December 1890, Lieutenant Bull Head, Sergeant Red Tomahawk, and a small party of Indian police, surrounded the cabin of Tatanka Yotanka (known to white Americans at the time, and generations of schoolboys thereafter, as Sitting Bull). The old Hunkpapa chief was shaken out of his sleep and put under close arrest. As Tatanka Yotanka was led from his cabin to his horse, a crowd of reservation Indians gathered; determined to set him free. In the scuffle which followed, shots rang out and the old chief was shot in the head. At such close range the bullet smashed a bloody hole in his skull the size of a saucer.

At the sound of gunfire, Tatanka Yotanka's white stallion - a gift from Buffalo Bill Cody - began to go through it's old circus routine. For a long moment the crowd fell silent.

They thought they were witness to a miracle.

They thought the horse was doing the Ghost Dance.

To the white man, Tatanka Yotanka's 'crimes' were many: not least the slaughter of the arrogant and stupid Yellow Hair at Little Big Horn. But the 'crime' which led to his death, was one in which he was only peripherally interested.

The Ghost Dance began on the west coast, with the emergence of the Indian Messiah, Wovoka; a Paiute Indian who allegedly carried the stigmata. Wovoka instructed his followers to dance the Ghost Dance in preparation for the return of their ancestors; in preparation for the passing away of the white man in a great earth wave. At the end, the white man had left the Indian nation little more than dreams and dancing.

But the white man did not understand the Ghost Dance. It frightened them; they sought out the ring-leaders. Someone entered the name of Sitting Bull on a list. It was enough. They sent his own people to take him. And in the end, it was his own people who destroyed him. In the dirt outside his cabin. His eyes still bleary with sleep. In a pool of gore and mud.

Thus do dreams, sometimes, become a waking, bloody nightmare.

In England. At the end of the 1970's; almost a century later. Heavy-handed, bungled arrests, sparked off a wave of riots in St. Paul's, Bristol; Brixton, London; Moss Side, Manchester. It was a pattern which repeated itself over and over throughout the 'eighties. Almost always, the trigger was a cannabis arrest. Almost always, the suspects were young blacks. Nothing left but dreams and dancing. Ghost Dancing. Dream Dancing. Life goes on.

By the end of the decade, the scenes of rioting became almost a permanent

Strangeways Riot. The biggest House Party of the Eighties.
(by kind permission of Manchester Evening News).

feature on our television screens. Whole neighbourhoods were burned. Shops were smashed and looted. Police in helmets and riot shields, belaboured young looters with long night-sticks. And dodged bricks and petrol bombs. In London, one policeman was hacked to death with machetes. The sharp crack of gunfire echoed around the tenement slums. Not only in the streets. In football stadiums, the broken bottles and Stanley knives flashed, and splashed blood. The terraces filled with the weeping reek of tear gas. In Strangeways - and at other prison sites - the landings erupted with anger, in a whirling, screaming, slate-hurling orgy, of bitterness and destruction.

That same year, in a lengthy interview, plotting and analysing the impact upon the working classes of the agrarian and industrial revolutions; the First and Second World Wars; the depression in the 'thirties; and Wilson's white heat of technology, Marxist historian, Professor Hobsbawm, was asked his opinion of the present situation. The Marxist analysis disappeared. The careful, structured dialectics were put to one side: for the moment. "Ah yes", quoth the worthy professor, "the descent into barbarism". Norman McCaig recalls, that Hugh MacDiarmid once informed him that 'dialectics' was the art of believing two opposing views at the same time. Perhaps the great bard was right. Marxist analysis was left, at last, speechless (save for slogans), paralysed, ineffectual. Once more, the Hun were at the gates of Rome.

England had slumbered for a decade. It was a rude awakening. The policies of monetarism were tearing the heart out of the decaying inner-cities. Between 1979 and 1981, *recorded* unemployment had doubled to 3 million. For many young people in the inner-cities, there was nothing left but dreams and dancing.

Around the world, things were changing at a dramatic pace. The Americans had got out of Vietnam. The Russians had got into Afganistan. In Iran, (the Daily Telegraph was still, resolutely, calling it Persia) the Shah had been deposed and the new fundamentalist Islamic government had outlawed domestic use of opium with brutal and bloody sanctions. In Pakistan, only a few years previously, a similar, though military-led, fundamentalist government had deposed and executed Bhutto. Lebanon was burning. Wherever you were in the Middle East at the start of the 'eighties, expressing your inner self through the 'glorious poppy' was a risky business.

All that heroin. All labbed up and no place to go. Except westward. Except into Europe. Except into England. England was ripe for it. Sweet slumbering England. With its established distribution systems. With its urge for the exotic. With its handy Middle Eastern connections. With its unemployed. Heroin, as the man said, is not ideal for the unemployed: but the unemployed are certainly ideal for heroin.

In the drugs field, some of us had said it would happen. But I don't think that we had really believed it. We had pointed to the steady increase in recorded heroin users and muttered Domesday proclamations. But to see our predictions come true, probably surprised us more than anyone else in sleepy England. Suddenly, heroin was everywhere. The craze for smoking - probably an unfortunate correlation between a new awareness and a glut of less soluble Middle Eastern heroin - took everyone by surprise. Suddenly, everyone who had always wanted to know what all the fuss was about, but couldn't stand the idea of injecting, was offered the field. Come on down. Kick the ball around. What else were you planning to do between giros?

In Lifeline too, we had been showing signs of terminal fatigue. The verve and excitement had gone out of us. Our fascination with therapy was wearing thin. (One member of staff had badly damaged his back during a trust game. The idea was that he should fall from a window ledge; and the fact that we caught him would prove that he could trust us. In all sorts of other ways. With his personal problems. With his inner psyche. It was, you see, symbolic. Oh boy! We dropped him. We were close to dropping therapy altogether too). We were riven with political dissent and fresh out of ideas.

An excellent time for the Health Service to decide to emulate our fading practice! We were, I suppose all growing tired and disenchanted. I had begun to write theoretical articles on addiction for the academic press: a sure sign that we had little useful left to say.

We had leapt into bed on the first date with the Health Service and lay there purring like a fat cat that had avoided getting kicked out with the empty milk bottles. The Hun were at the gates of Rome once more, but we weren't with them. The Romans had discovered that we had some jolly interesting ethnic goatskins for sale. And us? Oh, we wanted all that civilisation. For a while, it seemed as if we were just growing old.

Our customers had grown old with us too. Some managed to carve out careers with the new heroin users, as dope testers. Others, Richard Branson/Felix Dennis-style learned to profit from the revolution. Branson and Dennis had become successful capitalists. Now some of the bleary-eyed 'Bohemians' of the 'seventies became dealers to the 'street-wise runts'. But most simply got tired, and either stopped using, or gave up the ghost.

Lenny hung himself in police custody. With his belt. When they came to cut him down, his shoulder-length hair had become trapped in the instrument of his termination. For a moment, they said, they had thought that he had hung himself by his hair. Like Absolom. But no doting David to cry for Lenny. No distraught father to weep. To don the sack-cloth and ashes. To write psalms; or poems; or songs. To tear his hair.

Just a bleak rain-slashed, unmarked hole in the ground. Just an ageing Roman Catholic priest who, wrongly briefed, had assumed he was dealing with, yet another, accidental overdose.

Some just began to wear away. Robbie went back to live with his older brother Dennis. Robbie had run the gauntlet. The big man at the Zanzibar coffee bar. The poet at the Left Wing Club. One of the first to take Prestwich Hospital's infamous electro-convulsive therapy route to a prescription for life, Robbie was now back in the bosom of the family.

Big brother Dennis had brought Robbie up in the 'fifties after their parents had died - or simply got bored and wandered away. And Dennis had brought up his younger brother. More or less. Now he and Robbie existed in an almost-derelict two-room council flat. In an almost naked-lunch symbiosis.

Dennis was in desperate need of a complete rewiring job. In and out of various psychiatric hospitals throughout the 'seventies, he was, by then, on nardil, a monoamine oxidase inhibitor. Not a bad life perhaps, if you had no deep-seated urge for cheese. Cheese was out. Definitely. Dennis had been warned. Given his medication, cheese could be a killer.

Dennis would occasionally appear, wild-eyed and dishevelled in the day-centre. He could be particularly distracting at lunch-time. Particularly if the free mid-day meal consisted (as it very often did - very often) of vegetables in cheese sauce. Dennis would hover inches in front of some unfortunate diner. "What you eating?", he'd say, "Uurgh, cheese sauce. D'y'know", he'd say, "if I was to eat that, I'd die. In minutes. Right here in front of you. On the floor. An 'orrible death it'd be. 'Orrible". Then he'd move on to someone else. "What you eating? Uurgh! cheese sauce . . . . .". Dennis had been warned.

Robbie had been warned too. But Robbie was looking for something to accelerate his downward spiral. Perhaps he was hoping to pass the 'sixties on the way down. To give a cheery wave. When he was asked to be the driver in a big heist, Robbie didn't hesitate. The plan involved stealing a lorry-load of British pharmaceutical heroin from a motorway service station. Robbie was to be the driver. When the great day (or rather, the great night) came, Robbie was directed to the wrong lorry. Only when he was halfway back to Manchester, did his fellow knights of crime reveal that he had actually stolen 15,000 pairs of Tuff boots. And they would be needing somewhere safe to stash them wouldn't they . . . . ?

Dennis was distraught when the footwear arrived in the middle of the night and filled the most dark, untouched recesses of his flat. (He checked his Freeman Hardy Home Shopping Catalogue, and confirmed that he had never ordered them). Not so distraught, though, as Robbie, who had been looking forward to an early Christmas for the past two weeks. Now at two o'clock in the morning, he began to feel distinctly sweaty. Very, very withdrawn.

Nothing daunted, Robbie took the stolen articulated lorry out to score something useful.

It took about ten minutes for Robbie to get picked up and busted. But the raid on the flat, later that morning, would have required a Spike Milligan script and Gerald Scarfe illustrations to do it any real justice.

Having kicked in the door, our boys in blue found themselves wading through 15,000 shoe boxes to the small kitchenette where Dennis confronted them. Making his last stand in front of the fridge, Dennis held aloft a half-pound of Cheddar, shouting; "Don't come any closer or I'll kill myself".

You had to be there, I suppose.

Still, these were but brief moments of glamour, (though not, perhaps for Robbie and Dennis). Most of the time, the growth of the new heroin culture in the 'eighties was vicious, desperate, unlovely and unexpected. Most of all - for us - unexpected. But there was in all this; in the drugs explosions, the music, the restlessness of the 'eighties, echoes of the past which the violence, the brutality, the abandonment of innocence could not entirely mask.

What was familiar about the 'eighties, was the rebirth of confusion. The rebirth of hallucinogenic drugs. The rebirth of rebirthing.

For those of us who cut our teeth on knowing the difference between mod dancing and beat dancing, between urban blues and rhythm 'n' blues, between ska and blue-beat; the close proximity of musical forms was nothing new. The idea that people younger than us might understand such things, (and that we might not), was not new; but depressing.

For a while, it seemed as if the 'eighties would be the nostalgia decade. Hovis sales began to look up. Bruce Springsteen - a sort of Neil Diamond with T-shirt and monkey wrench - became "the Boss". Madonna appeared; modelling herself upon earlier icons including Marilyn Monroe (though without the singing ability, or the cachet of having fucked two Kennedys), and Jean Harlow, Wall's ice cream cones, and Mae West (though without the biting asides). Morrisey acquired the tenancy of Lennie Cohen's old bed-sit and went straight out to the local Spar for a packet of razor blades.

Channel 4 secured a cult following by screening 'fifties and 'sixties television programmes; for both adults and children. Even 'Ready Steady Go' was rescreened. And to everyone's surprise, during the dark shadowy days of the 'seventies, the rights had been bought up by Dave Clark. Remember him? He was glad all over about the 'eighties.

"The Drugs too, became familiar again. Cocaine made a come-back and LSD".

The decade was filled with cover records of earlier 'sixties hits. The Smiths even released a single with Sandie Shaw.

The cult of the singer-songwriter made a comeback, with old hands including Bob Dylan, Joni Mitchell, Ted Hawkins, Richard Thompson touring again without the backing bands, and packing them in. Loudon Wainwright III secured a regular spot on Jasper Carrot's Saturday night television show. New faces appeared using the old formula. Michelle Shocked, Tracy Chapman, Billy Bragg. Even Elvis Costello went out without his Attractions.

The drugs too, became familiar again. Cocaine made a come-back. And LSD. And barbiturates (present in a surprising amount of street heroin seizures). And mandrax (in a similar supporting role as an adulterant - like a fading star, relegated to the lesser billings. Guesting for newer bands). Even methedrine made a tentative reappearance in some areas.

Most had never gone away. Even in their heyday in the 'sixties, some drugs could be more easily obtained 'out of town'. Eccles, Ashton or Stalybridge were always the best places to go for amphetamine sulphate. To a limited extent they have actually managed to maintain their position in the great game. Macclesfield was always methedrine town; though now it doesn't even make silk ties any more. Another legacy of the monetarist experiment.

But although things had an air of familiarity about them, really they were only joking. Really they were just winding up the wrinklies who thought they might be able to delouse the old Afghan and gain some serious cred with their kids.

Because what was happening was a generation apart from the upheavals of the 'sixties. It's real connection lay in the fact that it was a phenomenon, and, as such, attracted hordes of eager social scientists, deconstructionists, discourse analysts, reporters, post-modernists (themselves, products of the 'sixties revolution) to examine and speculate, to draw comparisons, to sift through the wreckage of the regular rat-tat of explosions. But in the end, it was *another event* and we weren't welcome or invited.

The off-spring of the summer of love had grown up. And they were going to have a party. MC Tunes told 'Smash Hits': "I was brought up a hippy. My mam was a hippy. I was wearing beaded headbands when I was six/seven months old. Me mam took me to Glastonbury when I was three. Jimi Hendrix was my favourite". The big hit Manchester Celtic band, Toss the Feathers featured both the son and nephew of the great Donegal fiddle player Des Donnelly. Gavan Whelan, one-time drummer with James, was the son of one of the pioneers of the Manchester folk revival of the 'sixties. In 1967, in the Magic Village, it is said, you could occasionally rub shoulders with John Mayall's dad. Life goes on.

And so the wheel turned. Football replaced eastern mysticism. The Hacienda

"Suddenly everyone knew what Leeds Fans meant by those 'LSD and two E's 'T' Shirts.

and The Boardwalk replaced the Twisted Wheel and the Oasis. And Manchester was really cooking again. Indie, rap, hip-hop, house. Musical styles merged, crashed, clashed, like continents in prehistory. The bands spewed out of the machine faster than taxi-firm cards drop through your letter box. The Smiths, James, 808 State, Kiss AMC, The Charlatans, The Stone Roses, Ruthless Rap Assassins, Inspiral Carpets, New Order, A Man Called Gerald, Northside, The Man From Delmonte, Happy Mondays.

Clubs too. The Boardwalk, Legends, Millionaires, International 2, The Hacienda. What was really new, though, was the proliferation of record labels and management companies. Bop, Playhard, Rough Trade, Ugly Man, Playtime, Factory and, maybe, hundreds more.

The link between football, fashion and music was new too. George Best had done it a little. Clubbing it, getting drunk, wearing paisley shirts. Before him, Albert Camus had played goal for Algeria. But 'The End' (the fanzine-readers fanzine) broke new ground in football literature; part charting, part promoting drugs, music and fashion literature on the terraces. The pages of The End - and a myriad of fanzines after - were filled with dispute about which trainers to wear, what kind of coats; what kind of trousers. And the debate on the relative virtues/naffness of Pringle or Perry tops: phew!

Arguably, the real surrealism began at Maine Road, where City fans waved inflatable bananas. Inflatables really caught on from then. By the time of the European Championships in Germany in 1988 almost every club in Britain seemed to have its inflatables craze. Altrincham fan and ex-Freshies member Chris Sievey did his bit when he emerged, in a mask, as Frank Sidebottom, with his single 'The Robins aren't Bobbins'. 'The End' (the magazine/fanzine) became The Farm (the band) and jammed on stage with Mick Jones; formerly of The Clash. Suddenly the connection was obvious. Suddenly it became clear just exactly what those 'On an Away Trip' banners really meant. Suddenly everyone knew what Leeds fans meant by those 'LSD and two E's' T-shirts. Another summer of love had started, and a bridge had been formed between the terraces and the clubs.

Don't hold your breath. Tears before bedtime are confidently predicted. A combination of Balearic Beat imported from Ibiza and 'house' music from Chicago's gay community were fused together (with a lot of other stuff) to create Acid House. Acid House transmuted into Rave and ushered in an open season on LSD, ecstasy, amphetamine and cannabis.

But how did it all begin? When did drug use kick off? Who was Pavlov? Will Manchester United ever win anything? Who put the bop in the bop-she-bop-she-bop? Sit down. Pull up a chair. Let me tell you a story.

CHAPTER SIX

WAKEY! WAKEY!

"What drugs did we use? Give over.
We used everything we could get our hands on.
So long as it was flavour of the month.
It hadn't got to be naff, see.
Someone'd say; 'have y'tried these and whoa!
Gimmee, gimmee, gimmee.
I started on speed in the Twisted Wheel and I'm still
bopping.
Ecstasy's alright though".

Anonymous Drug User
from
'Personal Communication'

From "Drugs Through the Ages"
Smack In The Eye, Issue 4

WAKEY! WAKEY!

My first memories of inspirational music were of those occasional guest appearances by Lonnie Donnegan on the Sunday afternoon Billy Cotton Band Show in the 1950's. Somewhere in between Alan Glaze's 'I Can't Do My Bally Bottom Button Up'. and Kathy Kirby's 'Once I Had A Secret Love' came ' Rock Island Line' and 'Cumberland Gap'. And that fairly made the bakelite and walnut veneer rattle and roll. The short-lived skiffle craze probably owed more to Ken Colyer; but Lonnie Donnegan had the hits. Coming out of the Chris Barber Jazz Band, Donnegan, almost single-handedly created the bridge between jazz and the later beat boom; and infected a nation's youth with an obsession for guitars. Suddenly, everyone had to have one. When, in 1958, the restrictions on hire-purchase arrangements were abolished, anyone who could persuade mum or dad to cough up the deposit, could kit themselves out with the equipment to start a group.

Jazz didn't die immediately, and in Manchester at least, jazz and beat co-existed throughout the early sixties. Often in the same venue. Often on the same bill. The 2J's and the Left Wing Coffee Club - both essential beatnik/jazz joints - hosted dual-music nights with beat support for their headliners like Acker Bilk, Chris Barber and so on. Both the 2J's and the Left Wing closed in the early 'sixties to be reincarnated as the Oasis and the Twisted Wheel respectively.

Of all the great partnerships - Morecambe and Wise, Mutt and Jeff, Lennon and McCartney, meat and two veg, Nixon and Watergate - probably, the combination of popular music and drugs has been the most denied, lauded, despised, analysed and fought over.

Whatever the facts about the relationship, one thing remains undeniable: young people in the early 'sixties dived headlong into both drugs and popular music, because both offered euphoria. Both offered, too, a pleasure palace to which the older generation - Leary, Trocchi and Kerouac notwithstanding - were not admitted.

By 1963, the twin cities of Manchester and Salford were buzzing with music. The list of clubs and coffee bars was almost endless. And the music was almost a twenty-four hour event. Jimmy Saville was hosting lunchtime jive sessions at the Plaza. A host of clubs where offering early-evening to early morning events; most with at least two live bands. Pubs held regular beat, or rock 'n' roll, evenings. And this was not confined to city centres. The Higher Broughton Assembly Ballroom; the Majestic Ballroom, Patricroft; the New Luxor Club, Hulme; Devil's Cave, Newton Heath, were all popular venues where, for a small admission price, you could see the best of Manchester's talent and a host of imports from all over the country. From abroad too; notably the USA. Little

Richard played the Domino Club, Openshaw. Two solid hours of rock 'n' roll mayhem with a pitched street battle thrown in for good measure afterwards.

Outside the twin cities, almost every town had at least one beat club and one coffee bar attracting hundreds of young people to see Freddie and the Dreamers, Johnny Peters and the Crestas, Hermans Hermits, the Hollies, the Emperors, the Toggery 5. There was the King's Hall in Cheadle, the Manor Lounge in Stockport, Club Creole in Wilmslow, El Rio's in Macclesfield. El Rio's hosted one of the first appearances of the Beatles in the area; with Wayne Fontana and the Jets as support. Macclesfields main hang-out coffee bar, the Cavendish (the Cav) served three kinds of coffee - espresso, Nescafe and flat Nescafe. Flat Nescafe was made with plain milk. No bubbles. For a time it was regarded as a very hip order.

It was a period when tastes in music, and in drugs, continually merged and drifted apart. When the Shangri-La's played the Manor Lounge, they attracted an audience of both mods and rockers. Despite the media hype, there was no real trouble; though when the group launched into their hit, 'Leader of the Pack', the rockers, who had been somewhat sulkily clustered at the back, unceremoniously shouldered aside the mod crowd to get at the stage.

The Twisted Wheel was not the first club to offer all-night sessions, but it remains one of the most vividly remembered. It spawned a legacy of imitators across the North West which continued for many years. All-nighters at the Wigan Casino continued for over a decade and were equally famous for the purity of their Northern Soul offerings and the quantity of amphetamine consumed.

Amphetamines and soul played an important part in that early music scene. Heroin and morphine were around too. They were fairly common currency in coffee bars such a the Zanzibar, the Mogambo and the Cona. Barbiturates and mandrax had their heyday at the end of the decade. The Heaven and Hell Club was famous for mandrax and sustained one of the earlier raids by the newly-formed drug squad (1967). Legend has it, that the officers came equipped with stepladders and 100 watt bulbs, since the club lighting was so dim that arrests in the semi-darkness would have been impossible.

Around that time too, the Magic Village - now buried somewhere under the monstrous Arndale centre - arose out of the ashes of the Cavern Club. The 'Village was the heart of psychedelia. A confusing maze of tunnels - in which it was possible to buy underground magazines such as 'OZ', 'IT', 'Black Dwarf' and Manchester's own 'Grass Eye' - led to a small, darkened auditorium with a permanent light show, where it was possible to hear poetry, have your mind altered by a variety of substances, pretend to be Jesus, or have your hearing damaged by the Edgar Broughton Blues Band. The Third Ear Band got so stoned there that, when someone stole their p.a. equipment, they decided it was a message from the divine spirit that they should go acoustic; and they stayed that way.

Religious crazes vied with drugs for the hearts and minds of the young. The Incredible String Band found Scientology and took many of their fans with them. Then there was the promotion of the Mahareshi Mahesh Yogi and his Transcendental Meditation, by the Beatles; a long-lived craze which resurfaced in 1992 with the involvement of the Natural Law Party in the General Election - financed mainly by George Harrison. In the early 'seventies, there came a succession of prophets and cults. The Hare Krisnas with their shaved heads, cow bells, orange robes and those improbable Hush Puppies. The Guru Maharaji (immortalised in 'Mole Express' - successor to 'Grass Eye' - as the Greasy Margarine Jerk) with his Divine Light Missions.

All at some point drew in the gullible, the lost, the hurt and distressed. Many were drug users. Nurtured through the 'sixties on a diet of Tolkein and ley lines, their orientation to the Orient was no great surprise. Some were practical about these involvements and saw them - like short prison sentences - as a break from the hurley burley of drug dependence. Some rehabilitation houses, and the Common Cold Research Centre, enjoyed a similar status in the drug users' personal holiday brochure. The Hare Krisna Temples, like the original Lifeline Project day centre, offered free food.

The Lifeline Project grew out of the Manchester coffee bar tradition. By 1970, three coffee bars played somewhat reluctant hosts to the drug-using community. The most important, in some ways, was the Baked Potato on New Brown Street, which was popular for it's proximity to the, newly-opened, alternative shop On the Eight day. Duncan Foster's Coffee Lounge, (handy for Boots the Chemist on Peter's Square, where most of those registered at the, newly-opened, Prestwich Hospital clinic picked up their prescriptions), is fondly remembered for the quality of its conveniences. Most significant for the Lifeline Project, was the Catacombs Coffee Bar Club; a Christian-based project which offered free admission to see "rhythm groups" and "the cheapest coffee in town".

The Catacombs was located on Back George Street, in the basement of the building on Moseley Street which was rented by Lifeline. For a short period, the two organisations co-existed in relative harmony. When the Catacombs closed down, the Lifeline Project occupied the additional space. I don't remember that we ever paid for it; we regarded it as having been liberated.

Some years later, during a major clean-out, we found a pile of old conversion cards. Volunteers at the Catacombs has been issued with these on a weekly basis. There were spaces to fill in the names of those who had converted to Christ that week. Whether they had made any confessions. Whether they had prayed. We all laughed. For quite a while. But in truth, we too, were affected with the same missionary disease. It's just that we didn't go in for those cable-knit sweaters. Or endless renderings of 'Streets of London' and 'Needle of Death'.

For a while the day centre operated the most unusual taxi service in town. The Baked Potato or On the Eighth Day would telephone to say that someone had collapsed on their premises and we would simply drive round, bundle them in and bring them back to Moseley Street. After a while the message started to get through and people would get stoned and come straight to us. It was a sort of Pavlovian process. Pavlov was the one who discovered he had an irresistible urge to feed dogs every time a bell rang. After a while the dogs got wise to it and began to ring the bell every few minutes. In a few short years, he frittered away the family fortune on Pedigree Chum Mixer. Life goes on.

By then, regular supplies of heroin and cocaine from general practitioners had all but dried up. Most of our customers were using barbiturates and mandrax, pepped up with occasional flurries of opiods such as pethidine, palfium, and later diconal. There was also a lot of LSD and some speed.

Diconal became particularly popular during the 'seventies. It was the shellac to heroin's French polish. It didn't require much application. It contained an anti-emetic, so it was possible to establish a habit without really trying. You rarely got sick with diconal. During 1976 a customer survey at Lifeline found that diconal was most people's first-choice drug; beating heroin, morphine and even cocaine. Cocaine mixed with heroin had a brief popularity in the 'sixties and early 'seventies. The mixture was given various titles including speedball, hot and cold, H and C. In Manchester it was often called simply, 'the full monty'.

Mixture drugs had always been popular. During the heady days of the Twisted Wheel, by far the most sought after pills were 'purple hearts', a combination of amphetamine and barbiturate. Currently, the new hit on the rave scene is an ecstasy concoction called 'rhubarb-and-custard' which contains pheno-barbitone and caffeine.

Diconal was put on a special license with heroin and cocaine, in the early 'eighties. Within two years, in parts of greater Manchester some drug users had discovered cyclizine, a travel sickness preparation, freely available over the counter. Cyclizine could be mixed with the opiod of your choice to create a diconal effect. Better. The cyclizine could be adjusted to personal preference, to provide just the right amount of anti-emetic. The cyclizine itself, had become a sought-after hit. Just think of that. Life goes on.

Throughout the early 'seventies, Manchester had gone into a major sulk. Mainly because the media insisted on talking about Merseybeat. Mainly because

From "The A-Z of Safer Sex"
Smack In The Eye, Issue 3

the Hollies never made it as big as the Beatles. (They weren't good enough. And they didn't write their own songs. And Herman's Hermits were crap. Lady Byrd Johnson is reputed to have said of Gerald Ford that she could make a better man out of a banana. She couldn't even have made a banana out of Herman).

Around the mid-seventies the city had its punk temper tantrum. The Buzzcocks and the Fall became the big local bands. The Buzzcocks rehearsed in the Lifeline day-centre. (So did Sad Cafe - big then; forgotten now). They even did a benefit for the organisation.

Punk was brash, aggressive and violently anti-music-business; and was therefore bought up in great gobfulls. By the music business. One of it's most visible features was a stage signature which involved spitting at the audience. It wasn't terribly original. During the 14-hour Technicolour Dream at the Alexandra palace in 1967, a group called the Flies opened theirs and peed on the audience. I should know. I was among those who got slightly wet. Golden Showers - later to be described in loving detail in a myriad safer-sex leaflets - has thus never held a particular attraction for me. Much earlier, Dylan Thomas had allegedly outraged American audiences in similar fashion. But, as the man said, I missed that gig.

The punks took to the newly rejuvenated glue-sniffing craze with gusto. It offered exactly the right amount of euphoria, mixed with apparent self-degradation, that the new nihilistic craze demanded. This, too, was not new. Solvent sniffing apparently began in America, during prohibition when many American citizens, deprived of the world's favourite drug had taken to sniffing petrol. Extensive media coverage, finger-wagging police activity and the inevitable community outrage, led to widespread restrictions on the sale of solvent-based glues. This, in turn, led to a switch by many young people to the far more dangerous practice of sniffing aerosols.

The punk revolution didn't last for very long. Like the psychedelia of the 'sixties and skiffle in the late 'fifties, it was sucked in, polished, stroked, tickled, pumped up, neutered and sold. But like it's predecessors, it put a firecracker up the arse of complacency. Punk was the raw, angry, disaffected, unemployed, homeless, snarling, bitter preface to the Thatcher revolution. And it scared the pants off the politicians. Some punks graduated onto blackmarket heroin which found its way onto the streets of most cities in the UK at around that time. Prior to that, most of the heroin available to the young drug-using community came via burgled chemists and pharmaceutical warehouses. Some came from corrupt doctors; usually by recycling drugs legitimately prescribed in cases of terminal illness. On 2nd February 1979 Sid Vicious died in New York of a heroin overdose. Evo-stik to needlestick. Sometimes it feels that not much changes.

The sudden explosion of heroin in England, (and to lesser extent, in Scotland and Wales also), made drug use, once more the sort of political issue it had once been in the late 'sixties. In the main it was heroin. Increasingly smoked (or tooted) by unemployed, angry, working class kids. It was given a substantial marketing boost by the Government's 'Heroin Screws You Up' campaign.

But, behind all the hype, something really scary was happening. As the late 'seventies gave way to the next decade, the distribution of heroin was becoming much more organised. More ruthless. More criminal. Small user-dealer networks gave way to more organised retailing; using rented apartments rather than domestic homes. Using 'runners' as intermediaries. Using mobile phones. Using hand-guns and other weaponry.

One pair of dealers, working out of a high-rise apartment (working; not living), became very active in their local tenants' action group, petitioning and campaigning for an effective entry phone system for security purposes. Security had a particular importance to them. Territory was important too. The late 'eighties and early 'nineties in Manchester were marked by gangland-style shoot-outs, which filled the socks of some of the ravers out for a good time at International 2, and temporarily closed the Hacienda.

Moss Side was awash with drugs, violence, guns and reporters. There was an uncomfortable, insidious racist undercurrent to the press interest. Moss Side is a predominantly black area. During the late 'seventies, much of the heroin distribution in Manchester had been in the hands of organised crime syndicates, and nobody paid too much attention. Now, it seemed, it was in the hands of young blacks in Planet Ghetto and everyone had to sit up. After all, you could never be sure what those chaps might do. Could you? Increasingly, the police came under fire for making the area an unofficial 'no-go' zone. But the police couldn't win. Whilst it is probably true that drug dealing would not have been allowed to flourish in Altrincham Shopping Parade in the way it did in Moss Side Precinct, the police had come under fire in the aftermath of the riots, a few years previously, for being too eager to make drug arrests. For them, it must have seemed there was no way out. As Tommy Docherty remarked upon being dismissed by Preston North End: "As one door closes behind you, another slams shut in your face".

But the violence *was* frightening. Even the name 'Precinct' has a bloody, snarling New York ring to it. Increasingly, over the next few years, other areas of the twin cities -Cheetham Hill, Miles Platting, Ordsall etc. - began to muscle in on the act. First with heroin, then cocaine and crack; more recently the lush pastures of ecstasy sales. And the violence continues unabated.

By the middle of the 'eighties, the biggest advertising campaign of the decade was just beginning to wind up. Cocaine, we were told, was coming back. It was so great that you shouldn't even try it once. Douglas Hurd was against it. Like heroin, it was now available in smokable form. It had devastated the youth of America. It was so powerful that you could get hooked by just looking at it. Peter Townshend was against it. It was so fast that even David Mellor couldn't catch it in a Miami speedboat. David Mellor was against it. It was coming soon (but not yet). When it did come, it would be bigger than Elvis Presley. Elvis Presley was against it (or he would have been).

With an advertising campaign like that, you could sell 'cold turkey' in a Merseyside drug clinic.

But cocaine was an awful tease. Cocaine took its time. It took the best part of the decade before it really established itself: and by then much of the glamour had worn off the marketing image. One of the problems for the cocaine trade was that the North West had enjoyed a burgeoning trade in amphetamines since the 'fifties. Amphetamine sulphate was cheap, high in purity, long in effect, a well known product, used by your mates. Cocaine was expensive, low in purity, short in effect, an unknown quantity, used by Yanks and soft southern gits. Selling cocaine to speed freaks (and for a long time, hardly anyone else seemed likely to be interested) was always going to be like selling a Sinclair C5 to Hell's Angels. And then, something else happened.

I once watched two drivers clip wing mirrors. Both drivers stopped. One flung open his car door and rushed across the road to remonstrate with the other. In the middle of a heated argument, a third car, travelling at speed, swept round the corner and demolished the still open door.

It was a little like that. Everyone was watching cocaine (and heroin) when along came ecstasy. Suddenly, from nowhere; it was everywhere.

Almost without anybody noticing, drugs, music and popular culture began to merge. Began to jam with each other.

Throughout the 'eighties, the age at which people were recruited into heroin raced downwards at a dizzying pace. Towards the end of the decade, fears about the spread of the HIV virus and the levels of drug-related crime led to more 'flexible' prescribing. This was doctor-code for making it easier for drug users to secure a prescription for methadone. This meant more prescriptions, dispensed over longer periods. The argument runs, that by reducing dependence on blackmarket heroin, you reduce the incidence of acquisitive crime perpetrated to finance a drug habit. Enough prescribing might undermine the blackmarket. The availability of free drugs ensures that drug users stay in contact with services for longer and can therefore be prevailed upon to engage in safer injecting and sexual practices.

We found that young people would sit up and pay attention to Health Education messages if they were approached in the right way!

These arguments are not new. They are, in large part, an echo of the report of the Brain Committee in 1965. Then, appalled at the possibility of an emerging American-style blackmarket, the Committee recommended a toughening of the laws to deter the experimenters, and those who wilfully remained outside state control, in conjunction with maintenance prescribing for those who were already addicted.

Then, as now, the concentration was almost exclusively on heroin and a limited number of other drugs. Then as now, the policy was undermined by the emergence of a craze for drugs which, effectively, lay outside their remit. Then, it was barbiturates and mandrax. Now, it's ecstasy and LSD.

Ecstasy is not new. As MDMA, it was known to a small, and exclusive coterie of acid freaks in the early 'sixties. Leary used it and, reputedly, R.D. Laing. One dedicated user described it as "illustrated speed; methedine with pictures". It enjoyed a brief popularity with the herb tea drinkers at Gandalf's Garden, where it was used as an exotic new mode of transport to convey the initiated to Tolkein's Middle Earth. It was rarely seen outside London and had almost entirely disappeared by 1967. It was no competition - in those mellower days - for LSD; the big market leader.

But in the late 'eighties, ecstasy took off with a bang. It arrived, a little breathless, just in time for the second summer of love. "Hey, man, sorry I'm late. You guys been groovin' here long?". This time, it was LSD that was forced to wear the 'plus special guests' badge and sit outside with a bottle of tizer and a bag of crisps. By the start of the 'nineties, it had become clear that young people were 'on one' in numbers which simply dwarfed even our most pessimistic estimates of heroin use.

The downward spiral of heroin recruitment had slowed to a trickle. Ecstasy, LSD, amphetamine and cannabis had become the favourite drugs of the 'nineties children. These were party drugs. These were stand-on-the-terraces-and-shout drugs. These were dance-till-you-drop drugs. Ghost dancing. Dream dancing.

That was when Peanut Pete walked into our lives. We had already begun to emphasise, and concentrate upon, our work with younger drug users. All the figures showed that this was the group which was being missed by other services. Using the expertise which had been developed through the comic, 'Smack in the Eye', we began to publish handbill-sized comic leaflets aimed at providing accurate up-to-date information to users of rave-culture drugs. In most of the leaflets, Peanut Pete was a central character. An anti-hero, a smart guy (sometimes), a nurd (most of the time). Just like the real ecstasy users, he lives for the weekends. Just like the real ecstasy users, he sees himself as a million miles away from 'junkies' and the drug services that cater for them.

Dream dancing at the end-of-the-century Party. Where to in the 21st Century?

Once again, we found we had pressed just the right button. Lifeline's Manchester centre was inundated by young volunteers anxious to do almost anything: distribute our leaflets at rave nights, answer the phones, take photographs, make videos, process leaflet orders. Moving from dependent, to more recreational users meant big changes for Lifeline Manchester. The move towards a more consumer advice-style orientation - usually through telephone contact - was inevitable given the numbers of young people involved and the nature of their involvement.

In the life-cycle of any drug - of any group of drug users - there is always a honeymoon period. In the early 'sixties there was a time when you could use heroin, supplied by friends, and sit around the Zanzibar coffee bar and jaw about Kerouac and Charlie Parker. In the middle 'sixties there was a time when friends would turn on you. When the acid was good. When the mode of the music matched the spirit of the times. Matched the purity of the high. But "when the modes of music change, the laws of the state always change with them". And so do the operations of the rip-off merchants, the pimps, the hustlers, the snarlers, the shot-gun sharks. There comes a time when there's more talc than heroin, more strychnine than acid, more caffeine than ecstasy. There comes a time when the purity turns to water like the snow thaws in March. Then you wake one morning and the Christmas card is gone and you're back in the wastelands.

It doesn't have to be this way. For most it won't be. But when the mode of the music changes, some will be left behind. The flotsam of another orbit of popular culture. Spinning out of control on a trajectory which has ceased to exist. All alone on the dance-floor. Ghost dancing. Dream dancing. Life goes on.

CHAPTER SEVEN

POSTSCRIPT

"Ah, but l was so much older then
I'm younger than that now"

Bob Dylan
from
'My Back Pages'

POSTSCRIPT

Antoine Sainte-Exupery, in 'The Little Prince', *(the* 'sixties children's book), said that the whole population of the world could stand side by side on the Isle of Wight. He said that, if you told this to grown-ups, they would be unable to resist the urge to check your calculations. He was right. Of course. Here's another. From the Eastern tip of the Indonesian archipelago to its Western-most extremity is further than the distance from London to Bagdhad. Go ahead, check it out.

In the late 'sixties I worked with a middle-aged man from the Western Isles. peculiarly, he had a Spanish surname. When, one day I asked him how this came about, he explained that his ancestors had been with the remnant of the Spanish Armade which fled Northward. Battered by gales, they passed through the Pentland Firth and headed South again down the Western coast of Scotland. Here, the final disaster struck as they were shipwrecked upon a remote island. Speaking only Spanish, they would have had a hard time communicating with the island's Gaelic-speaking inhabitants. But Act of Union or no, they would have remained safe from their English pursuers. And they would have shared the same religion. It was a fascinating story, but it left one detail unclear. "How", I asked, "did you come to be called Emile? The surname I can understand, but surely the forename . . . . " Ach man, that was only a few generations ago!". And, I suppose, it was. Time and distance can be deceptive. Some things seem to have happened only yesterday. Others, seem buried almost beyond recall.

"Reminiscences", said George Bernard Shaw, "make one feel so so deliciously aged and sad". He didn't mention their tendency to remind you how stupid you must have been. Their capacity to embarrass. Unlike me, George Bernard Shaw was a vegetarian. Unlike me, George Bernard Shaw was tee-total. Perhaps it's just the red meat and alcohol.

A hundred years ago, it seems, I blew into the city and out of the rain. I was an angry young man. Filled with dreams. And hope. Anxious to be a part of great changes which would alter the face of the world forever. Now. Only the anger remains.

Mostly, it's about the missed chances and blind alleys. We spent our first ten years trying to wrest the dead hand of medicine off the drug treatment industry. We argued that the response to drug use - to pain and despair - should be about caring and community action. Should not be about social control through psychiatry. But when the medical profession started cooing in our direction we began to preen ourselves outrageously and fell off our perch.

For a short while, it seemed as if things really were changing. A flurry of new drug services were modelling themselves upon organisations such as ours. Prescribing was a very small part of the facilities they offered. Then, the mode of

Medicine, once again, steps centre-stage. With crime escalating dramatically even some Senior Police Officers have called for a limited form of drug legalisation. Neutering the street-wise runts, they argue, would produce a peace bonus with the ending of the War Against Drugs.

the music changed. Drug use began to rocket. Crime began to escalate. AIDS began to stalk the outer reaches of our world. Just outside the faint light of our camp-fire, it growled, coughed, rumbled. And services retreated once more into the safety of the tried and trusted practices. Under the shelter of the prescription pad. Medicine, once again, stepped centre-stage; smiled, benignly in the firelight.

I do not object to prescribing. I see no reason why drugs should not be used to ease the discomfort of withdrawal. Or to provide a period of stability in the lives of individual drug users. I do not even object to the notion of a prescription for life, *if that is what is in the best interests of the individual.* But increasingly this seems not to be the case. Increasingly, the decisions appear to hinge upon levels of crime in the community. Upon the risk of infection transmission into the 'wider' (read: non-junkie, non-scum) community. This, it seems to me, is a betrayal of trust. We have no political mandate to interpret and manipulate social policy. I believe it is also morally corrupt. Drug services are increasingly taking upon themselves an infection control remit which priorities the interests of society over those of the individual drug user.

On the occasion of our tenth anniversary, I wrote a report entitled 'Out From The Shadows'. On the penultimate page, I included a quotation from Thomas Bratter, discussing methadone maintenance in the USA:-

"Scientifically, until the medical issues regarding the short-and long-term physiological effects are answered, methadone maintenance remains an unproven enigma. Medically, to subject approximately 100,000 human begins to a potent chemical without proper controls, is malpractice of the most insidious sort. Legally, to imprison marijuana smokers and heroin addicts as criminally dangerous while concurrently maintaining that methadone addicts are law-abiding, is a travesty of justice. Philosophically, to confuse, deliberately, the concepts of 'treatment' and 'social control', is fraudulent. Psychologically, to convince addicts that there is a mystical metabolic disorder and that they must remain dependent on a potential poison rather than to strive for their autonomy, is a conspiracy. Ethically, any conspiracy which places people in 'no win' situations and mitigates against their growth and development, must be considered a criminal act".

I have changed my mind about a lot of things over the years. Sometimes, I have even changed it back again. But I can see no compelling reason to review my support for Thomas Bratter. In the last analysis, I believe that dependence upon mood-changing drugs is limiting to the human condition. In the last analysis, I hope that people will stop using before it hurts too much. It has of course been argued that long-term prescribing of substitute drugs will result in many being simply bored out of addiction. This too, is not a new argument. Sir Humphrey Rolleston used it in the 'twenties. I'm still waiting.

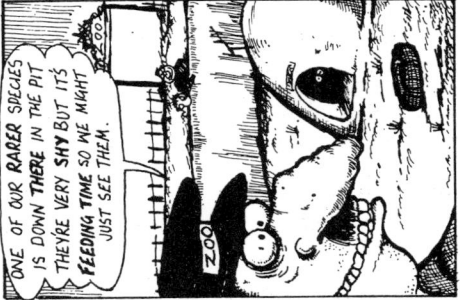

Smack In The Eye, Issue 8

Time, I suppose, will tell. Many researchers have noted a widespread tendency for drug users to mature out of addiction in their late-twenties. If this process, in years to come, appears to have been significantly undermined, then we will know. We will know that a policy which took the dangerous street-wise runts, neutered them, and left them at home on the sofa with a bottle of methadone and pap-television for company, has indeed had the effect of condemning many, who might otherwise have stopped, to a life on drugs. (Boring drugs, too). And it may be that society will feel that this is a price worth paying; for reducing the AIDS threat and the number of videos nicked out of urban households. But I don't think they've been asked. And I don't think that we have the right to take that decision without them. And, even if society did approve, don't expect me to like it. It's not why I started in this business, and I wouldn't find it a good reason to continue.

I had always hoped that, in a very small way, my involvement with the Lifeline project would prove to be a contribution to lasting change in the way we treated people whose lives had become consumed by drugs. Well, at least we don't give them ECT anymore.

Perhaps the real change has been in me. I'm a city slicker now; more likely to be found listening to the Baroque compositions of Bach and Handel, Boyce and Purcell than the pipes and fiddles of my youth. I suspect that I will never feel entirely comfortable with the suit, the collar and tie, but I know I look the part. I no longer feel it necessary to ensure that I have a penknife and a length of baling twine about my person at all times. Nowadays, I am more likely to be found with a briefcase filled with semi-pornographic comics and condoms. Some would say that this is progress.

But the progress is there for all that. I understand my icon now. I know what the dream was about. More than that. In this society, we entertain the odd notion that people who have been around for a long time in a particular sphere, might have something useful to say about it. This, despite all the evidence to the contrary. So my longevity, if nothing else, provides the Lifeline Project with a limited audience. In the early days, we struggled for an audience. Often, when we found one, it was hostile. Usually hurling abuse; occasionally other things beside. They were tough times to convince an angry and frightened public that drug users deserved a place in this society of ours. Hadn't they, after all, wilfully spurned the opportunities they had been offered?

Now, at least, we can speak and be heard. Even if what we say is derided. Even if what we say is uncomfortable. Now, at least, we can speak the dream above the din of voices. That drug users are owed our care and compassion *as a fundamental right*. That drug users are a part of the wider community; even if that same community insists on shuffling them out to the further reaches of it's periphery. That these rights and obligations remain, even without the fear and concern which currently motivate them. It would be easy to forget that these beliefs, twenty years ago, were howled down. Dismissed out of hand.

Every morning, when I arrive at work, I take the lift to the second floor. The lift is fitted with a full-length mirror. I try not to look. In the mirror, I can see that I have begun to grow old. Each morning, it seems, I'm growing older. Each month I go for a haircut. At the end of the operation, the barber holds up a mirror to the back of my head to ensure that I am satisfied with the parts I will never otherwise see. I'm too busy scanning the mirror for bald patches to notice the cut. As the hair thins, the waist thickens. My protestations about suffering from a receding chest, fall on deaf ears. My shirt now fits like Clayton Moore's Lone Ranger outfit. Twenty-one years ago, I arrived in Manchester for a fortnights holiday. For many years, I convinced myself it was a sojourn. One day soon I would return to where I belonged. Now, it's difficult to know *where* I belong. And all the time I'm growing older.

Recently, my son asked me if they had dinosaurs when I was a boy "in the olden days". No they didn't. But they had day centres where you had to set traps for the rats and mop out the back-up from the drains every morning. They had damp forbidding squats where drug users bathed with their socks on because that was the "easiest way to wash them". They had hippies and punks and barbiturates and diconal and heroin and airways and Roy Harper and vegetables in cheese sauce and riots and forged prescriptions and Salvation Army furniture and therapy and death and despair and hope and dreams.

And out of all of this we built an organisation. An organisation of which I am inordinately proud. An organisation that cares about the Little Billys; and the Sheilas; and the Maggies. An organisation that will continue to care about them even if they *don't* nick your video; or menace you with a life-threatening disease.

I have been accused of being arrogant. And bullish. And cynical. And uncompromising. It's true; I am. Perhaps not just me. Perhaps, these are the hallmarks of the Lifeline Project which we have created. And I hope it remains that way for the Little Billys; and the Sheilas; and the Maggies. In the end, there is no room for compromise; for half measures. Jimmy Melia, one-time manager of Brighton and Hove Albion, once remarked: "I expect players to see eye-to-eye with me. I certainly don't expect to have to see eye-to-eye with *them*".